how to

Write a
$aleable
Book

in 10-minute bursts of
MADNESS

"Be brave. Take risks. Blame no-one.
And amazing things happen."

Published by Next Century Publishing
Las Vegas, NV 89148

ISBN: 978-1-68102-002-0
Library of Congress Control Number: 2014920956
Printed in the United States of America
First printing August 2015

This book is dedicated to aspiring writers everywhere

The original version of this book was written in thirty-seven hours over twelve days, edited by a freelance editor in nineteen hours and designed, printed and delivered in four days.

It was launched for feedback at a Master Class for aspiring writers twenty-three days after I came up with the idea.

It took another six weeks to include feedback from the class, rework the structure and polish the pages and a further two months to complete this third, and final, draft.

Although *How to Write a Saleable Book in 10-Minute Bursts of Madness* focuses on writing a self-help book, the techniques, methodologies and exercises laid out in these pages lend themselves perfectly to other non-fiction genres including guide books, biographies, memoirs and most types of how-to books.

Acknowledgments

I love how one thing always leads to another.

Thanks to Barbara Hunt at the Ontario Writers' Conference for inviting me to give my first self-help writers' Master Class. My eternal gratitude goes to the extraordinary Dr. Marcie Kostenuik for getting back to me the day after attending the Master Class with pages of encouragement and really useful suggestions. My thanks to Rich Helms for making a bright light go on. And to my visionary friend, Ken Dunn of Next Century Publishing, for challenging the status quo and shaking up the publishing industry.

I'm indebted to Stacey Alper, a former publicist at Workman Publishing, and to Margo Herrera, a superstar editor at Workman, for sharing their expertise in these pages. Special thanks to Marie Lynn Hammond, my freelance editor on this project, for her sparkling logic and her written contribution.

And, as usual, to my wife Wendy—the most exciting and inspiring person I've ever met—for her unflagging support, her patience and her extraordinary eye for detail.

Contents

Once upon a time . . .

Yes, I'm starting this book with a story, because who can resist a good one? Besides, *"Once upon a time"* is a far more enticing heading than *"Introduction"* and, as you'll find out later, storytelling can make your self-help book come alive.

I'm going to tell you how I came to write my first self-help book, and how I, a complete non-writer, was actually able to pull it off! This story will also help you understand the passion, risks and resourcefulness required to write a self-help book from scratch, as well as show you the rewards in store for you when you succeed.

For many years I made a very good living as a photographer in the fashion business. In June 1994, I was invited to speak about my work at the North York Camera Club in Toronto.

"How can I make this interesting?" I wondered. "I know—I'll talk for five minutes about photography and fifty-five minutes about connecting with people. After all, that's what a fashion photographer does all day long."

When I'd finished my talk, three people came up to me: a doctor, a teacher and someone who trained airline personnel. "Can you come and give this talk to my people?" they each asked. "Not the photography bit, the rest. The connecting with people part."

That night I told my wife Wendy, "I've got a new job. No more jet lag and moody models, no more gossiping hair dressers and yawning assistants, and no more finding myself on a beach at five in the morning in the pouring rain waiting for the sun to appear! I'm going to be a speaker."

When I woke up the next morning, Wendy asked me, "Still want to be a speaker?"

"Yes, I do."

"So, now what?" she asked.

"I'm not sure yet."

"Why not treat organizing a speaking engagement as if it were a photo shoot?" She replied. "If you were hired to do a shoot of a speaker with an audience, what would you do?"

"Simple. I'd book some space at a local hotel and invite a bunch of people to come and listen."

"Well, what are you waiting for?"

By noon that day, I'd rented half of the ballroom at our local Holiday Inn for a date two weeks from then and invited a bunch of friends, clients, models and suppliers to come and hear me talk about "Rapport by Design," which is the title I came up with for my approach to connecting with people.

"Twenty-nine bucks a head," I told them, "and bring your friends."

My photo shoots were always a lot of fun, and I guess they thought my speech would be too. Whatever the reason, over eighty people showed up. I was buzzed. The event was a success.

I started talking to anyone who'd listen—Rotary Clubs, associations, networking groups—but my progress up the speaking ladder was slow. A model I knew had a contact at a hot TV show in Toronto called *Breakfast Television*. I wangled my way on.

It was March, so I talked to kids looking for summer jobs about the value of people skills. I offered to go to any school and talk to job-seeking students about interviewing skills for free. By the end of the day, nine schools had agreed to have me come, and in only a month, I spoke to 1,400 kids.

But my new speaking career was still moving too slowly for me, and because I'd pushed my photography aside, my income was taking a nosedive. What was missing? I reviewed my resources, and it hit me like a champagne cork. A book! And preferably a best seller with a killer title.

I traded in my cameras for a laptop and started to write—but I didn't have a clue where to start. Then a couple of things happened that changed everything.

The editor of our village newspaper stopped me outside the bakery and said she'd seen me on *Breakfast Television*. "Why don't you write an article for the paper about making people like you?" she asked.

Why not? I figured an article might even form the basis of a chapter for my book. The first article came so easily, I wrote a second. Both later became chapters.

The following week, a friend invited me to speak about "Rapport by Design" at an environmental fair she was promoting. In the afternoon, my friend told me she'd convinced the guy from the nightly news to talk to me about my book.

I was excited to see him and his cameraman approach. He came right up and said, "I hear you're writing a book."

"Yes," I said proudly.

"So, what's it called?"

"It's about rapport by design."

"Oh," he said and all the energy drained from his face. "And what's it about?"

"How to make people like you in about ninety seconds," I chirped out of nowhere.

"Nice," he said and the energy returned.

Then I added with a flourish, "Or less!"

"Love it. Got it," he said. "What's the point of your book?"

"When people like you, they see the best in you and they look for opportunities to say 'yes' to you. And, they make that decision in the first few seconds of seeing you."

"How am I doing then?" he said, flirting with the camera.

"Oh, yes," I said. "I like you already."

"Well, there you have it, folks! How to make people like you in ninety seconds."

"*How to Make People Like You in 90 Seconds or Less*," I chimed back.

"When is it coming out?" he asked.

"Soon." I said.

Perfect! I'd found my killer title.

My beliefs were confirmed three days later when I got a call from the acquisitions editor of a well-known Canadian publishing house. Their president had seen me on TV and was offering to buy the world rights for *How to Make People Like You in 90 Seconds or Less*.

"But I haven't written it yet." I said.

"Don't worry about that," the publisher said. "We'll take care of it!"

It was tempting because I was running out of money fast, but I thanked him and turned down his offer. But I had learned a valuable lesson about the power of a killer title in the self-help book world.

Energized, I wrote with a vengeance for the next three weeks. Then I got a call to speak at a Substitute Teachers' conference. They too had seen me on *Breakfast Television*. "Bring copies of your book," they urged.

"That's it. Enough writing." I cleaned up my manuscript and persuaded a local printer to run off 200 copies. He agreed to let me pay him the $400 at the end of the month.

My wife and I arrived at the conference looking amazing, Wendy in her $2,000 emerald green Escada jacket and me in my Hugo Boss suit—leftovers from the good old days. No one would have believed we were flat broke.

Wendy set up a table outside the room where I was speaking. We'd agreed to charge ten dollars a copy—if anyone was interested.

At the end of my talk a woman came over and asked if she could take my photo.

"Sure," I said.

"No, not here. Outside by the line at the book table."

The line stretched down the corridor and around the corner. Wendy and I could barely look each other in the eye for fear of giggling. We sold every copy except for fifteen books I slipped into my briefcase.

The next day, I mailed fourteen of them to different literary agents in the States and put the remaining copy in my desk.

Ten days later, I got a call from an agent who had sold my book to a huge American publisher. That little book put me on a whole new career trajectory.

I was fifty-two, and I was back.

Moral of the story? If I can write a book that sells, even though I'd never done it before, so can you! Oh, and never turn down an invitation to speak about photography at your local camera club, because opportunities are everywhere—and one thing always leads to another.

Why is this book different?

The problem for many would-be writers is that they never get started on their book. Or if they do get started, they never finish—or they slow down in the middle, procrastinate and lose interest.

How to Write a Saleable Self-Help Book in 10-Minute Bursts of Madness shows you how to prepare for racing from the beginning to the end of your book and then lay down an entire, ten chapter, first draft in about two weeks. It's pretty hard to get bogged down or discouraged in just fourteen days! In our accelerated workshops we achieve this in a single weekend.

Even better, this book asks you to invest a minimum of only thirty minutes a day, in ten-minute bursts, to produce a complete, albeit slightly naked, book. That's the hardest part of writing a book, and you get it out of the way fast. Along the way, you'll learn what separates books that sell from those that don't.

The next step—polishing your book—is the fun part. Once you know where you're going, puffing up barebones paragraphs with word pictures, sensory details, stories and examples is relatively easy. You can work on that after supper, during your commute, or in your favorite café.

Completing the more challenging part—laying down the framework—in those easy ten-minute bursts, while at the same time preparing the saleable elements, is what sets this book apart from the competition.

What's ahead?

This is not just a book about cutting through procrastination and hesitation and getting your whole book down on paper; it's a book about assembling the five elements of a book that sells: Preparing, Producing, Polishing, Promoting and Publishing.

Part One – Preparing

Before we get to the *how*, we need to look at the *why*: why write another self-help book, and why your particular book and topic? Even non-writers like me can become writers, and this part shows you how. And since we're all stuck for time, we start by writing in short bursts of madness, directly from your unconscious mind. Once you get this part down, you can watch the ideas flow!

Part Two – Producing

This is where you build ten "key" chapters as a framework for your self-help book. A Key Chapter is a first fast draft of a full chapter comprising a strong, focused, outline captured in three ten-minute burst of *Writing Madly*.

Part Three – Polishing

Next you polish your book and bring it alive by fleshing out the Key Chapters and connecting with your readers' emotions by adding anecdotes, short stories and exercises to illustrate your steps and points.

Part Four – Publishing and Promoting

The book publishing landscape for new authors is changing on a daily basis, but the role of book proposals, literary agents and publicists are components of book publishing that every writer needs to know, whether you choose to self-publish or look for a traditional publisher.

Finally we look at the options you have to promote your book, build your brand and even, as I did, reinvent your life. We look at the role lucky breaks and chance encounters play in your future success.

Appendix

Here you'll find 3 examples of 10-minute bursts of *Writing Madly*, as well as an overview and a table of contents from one of my books. These examples will give you ideas when you're structuring your own book.

Please read this carefully

Many of the techniques in this book are based in Neuro-Linguistic Programming (NLP). They are intended to bring about rapid advances in several different skill sets at the same time. Some skills are personal, like curiosity, empathy and imagination. Others are technical, like structure, crafting and pitching. Yet others connect with the emotions, like STORYspeak.

Along the way, you'll find a series of tried and tested exercises. These exercises follow a strict order, and each one comes with time limits and instructions. Feel free to do more than one day's work at a time, as long as you don't take shortcuts, omit exercises or fail to write everything down in the time that is requested of you.

You'll need a binder to store all your exercise notes and printouts, a pen, paper, a laptop or tablet, a timing device and a place where you won't be disturbed. **All exercise answers and notes must end up in electronic form by page 98.**

You will also find notes from my first book, *How to Make People Like You in 90 Seconds or Less*, to use as a case study along with notes for my next book. In this way, I can illustrate my points and make it easy for you to see how you can apply these steps to your own book.

My notes begin on page 45.

PART ONE: PREPARING

Writing a book and selling a book are completely separate undertakings. If you get the selling part right, before the writing part happens, your chances of success go through the roof.

The biggest little secret of a saleable book is to know who your primary audience is. It is not, as most people think, your reader. It's the book reviewers and bloggers, the bookstore buyers, the magazine editors, the radio and TV segment producers and all the other social influencers who impact the lives of millions through their work.

If you don't appeal to these very important people first, no-one, outside of your family and friends, is going to know your book even exists.

This requires preparation.

Chapter 1
The self-help world

Most of us wish we could improve the world around us. For the disillusioned lawyer, it might be a way to help the poor. For the ambitious social climber, it could be throwing the perfect dinner party. For the twelve-year-old boy with a social conscience, it might be teaching adults how to give back to the global community. For the brilliant scientist, perhaps it's sharing her technical wisdom.

Whatever the need, chances are there's already a book out there to show you how. Whether it's shedding shyness, eating less, exercising more, dancing flamenco, flying an ultra light from Cape Town to Sydney, or making people like you in ninety seconds or less, someone's probably beaten you to it.

So, why should you bother writing another self-help book? Why go through all the hours of writing, waking up in the middle of the night to scribble thoughts on scraps of paper, or banging away to finish a chapter only to realize it was fun to write but totally off topic? Why go through those days when you feel like you're running a marathon backwards on your hands and knees?

Help others, help yourself

Here's why you should bother: because a self-help book written by a credible author is like a magic wand and a bunch of ambassadors at the writer's beck and call twenty-four hours a day, all rolled into one. Your book can sell your expertise, build your brand and do your PR work, even while you're sleeping. It's your calling card, a demonstration of your worth and part of your legacy. Its potential to open doors is almost unlimited.

Every so often someone asks, "Hey, Nick, why do you call it a saleable book and not a sellable book?" There's an important distinction. If something is "sellable," it means it is fit to sell. A broken plate or toaster is not fit to sell. If something is "saleable," it means it has the potential for profit.

Your self-help book has the potential for profit. By revealing the wealth of expertise, experience and passion that's stuffed inside your head, your saleable book lets the world know you are an expert. It gives you instant credibility and respect. What's more, people will pay you handsomely to share your expertise.

Having trouble sleeping? Can't cope with your kids? Want to improve your love life? Stuck in a rut at work? Want to grow organic strawberries? Almost half the population has grabbed a book to help solve their problems and better their lives at some time in the recent past.

Self-help books have been around since 1859 when Samuel Smiles published the first personal development, self-help book called *Self-Help*. It began: "Heaven helps those who help themselves."

What is new is the scale and variety of the business today. Self-improvement book sales exceed $2.5 billion a year in the U.S. alone, and there's no sign of this slowing down. There are currently 345,227 self-help titles listed on Amazon alone.

Once you have a book, the sales it generates are just the beginning. A successful self-help author can substantially increase his or her income giving speeches and workshops. With fees ranging from $500 to $10,000 per speech (and lots more if you're famous or have a best seller), corporations, colleges and associations can make sharing your expertise in person a very tempting proposition.

Well-written self-help books by media-friendly authors typically sell well in the marketplace and are a favorite of literary agents and publishers.

But here's the catch. With almost one million books published in 2014 in the United States alone, yours can't be just another book, because anyone can write and publish a self-help book. Your book has to be special. It has to stand out from the rest. It must be different, fresher, more current than what's already out there. It needs an appealing voice and a new approach.

Who, what, why and how

It's also paramount that you know *who* you're writing for. Do you have a definable market, like left-handed golfers or owners of problem dogs, and how large is that market?

Also, *what* unique benefit does your book offer the reader that other books in your category do not? A benefit in this context is anything that makes your reader's life better, faster, cheaper, friendlier, sexier, richer, tastier, longer, happier, thinner, smarter, quieter, funnier—you name it.

In other words, you need to know *why* a reader would pick up your book instead of another one on the same topic, and *who* that reader is.

So, ask yourself, "*What* does my reader want and *how* will they know when they've got it?"

The overarching answer in any top-notch self-help book is he, or she, wants to be entertained and receive tools they can use immediately. That means your book must be liberally sprinkled with anecdotes and really useful, practical, hands-on exercises: invented or re-invented by you the author.

What publishers and the public are looking for

Publishers, on behalf of the public, are all looking for the next mega best seller, and the bigger companies all have acquisitions editors. As the name implies, their job is to acquire manuscripts for their publishing house. That means they know what sort of books work for them. They stay in touch with agents, read proposals and meet face to face with authors. Acquisitions editors are very busy people and don't have time to waste. The following advice was generously provided by my own editor at Workman Publishing in New York.

"I look for a book that offers **a promise** and delivers on it. If a person has a 'problem' they need help with (an irascible toddler, a boring dinner repertoire, an unclear sense of personal finance, resentful stepchildren, too much clutter), your book must help solve the problem."

"It's important that the **audience** know they have **the problem** and be seeking help—so they'll go to the bookstore or online to find help. I got a solid proposal on personal finance for middle-aged women," my editor recounts, "that would prevent poverty in older age (a real problem). But we didn't move forward on it because that audience doesn't know they need it. Only later on, when they're in financial trouble, will they look for help."

"I'm looking for the following: **substance, excellently written**. You can tell when you're getting good, solid information," she says, "and you appreciate it. It's important to express your ideas in an organized, clear, succinct, lively way. You need to have enough real information to warrant a book, rather than, say, a magazine article. You need it organized in a way that naturally carries the reader through. You need to make your points clearly once, maybe twice, but not repeat the same ideas over and over again."

"**A fresh take.** This can take many forms—a lively, irreverent voice and excellent writing; new expertise on a topic, new solutions; a unique new way of presenting material. For example, *How to Make People Like You in 90 Seconds or Less* brings the time component to a much-covered topic."

"**A highly publicizable author with energy and ideas.** A book's best advocate is its author. If someone has a fantastic platform and lots of fans, even if their book idea is nothing stellar, their popularity can sometimes make it work. Likewise, if someone is very energetic, passionate, mediagenic and hardworking—willing to promote their own work from many angles—that can help a lot."

Publishers, and the public, are hungry for fads. Just as in the seventies they wanted books about macramé and growing veggies, today they're hungry for crafts, magic, oceans and mind-benders.

As a self-help author, you must focus on your readers' problems and figure out how you can apply your knowledge, skills and expertise to solve these problems. As an expert, you must be prepared to continually improve and be at the forefront of your specialty. True experts invest lots of time and effort into growing, refining and innovating their expertise.

If you want to sell your book and get it noticed, you need to start working on your credentials and your credibility at the same time as you start writing it.

Chapter 2
You are more powerful than you know

We come into this world with nothing. Except for our five, natural-born *SuperPowers*. By SuperPowers I don't mean being able to leap over tall buildings like Superman; we have machines that can do that. I'm referring to our uniquely human abilities of enthusiasm, curiosity, the ability to process feedback, empathy and imagination. These five SuperPowers are everything we need to challenge the status quo, shake things up and write a book.

Over the years though, our SuperPowers take a buffeting and get out of whack; some fizzle out completely. We lose our childlike curiosity, our horizons become obscured by our habits, our empathy gets numbed by the nightly news, and our imagination ends up fueled by fear, leaving us in no shape to write a book.

It takes a special kind of passion and energy to challenge the status quo and shake things up. Al Pacino summed it up recently in an interview when Charlie Rose asked him, "How come you got all those amazing roles when thousands of other actors wanted the same roles?" "Because I didn't want them," Pacino replied. "I had to have them."

When you think about it, our most inspired, creative and productive acts occur when we HAVE TO HAVE something. With this unstoppable hunger our five SuperPowers combine and flow in timeless union—and in those rare precious moments, we literally buzz with certainty, purpose and energy. The French call this *joie de vivre,* or "the joy of living." In English, we call it vitality or high spirits or radiance or energy. The ancient Greeks had a better word for it: *enthusiasm.*

#1. enthusiasm

Nothing worthwhile is ever achieved without enthusiasm. It is SuperPower number 1, and we arrive in this world hooting and hollering and bursting with a passion for life. That's what the word *enthusiasm* means, "life flowing through."

It's important to distinguish between motivation and inspiration. Motivation comes from the outside in the form of sticks, carrots and accolades. Inspiration comes from the inside in the form of natural, unstoppable energy, or enthusiasm.

With enthusiasm you can inspire yourself and others to great heights. Without it there is no ambition, no great work, no passion. No book.

#2. curiosity

Curiosity, the ability to learn as we go, is a human survival skill. From the moment we are born, we start to look around and take in what's happening around us.

With curiosity you can explore and learn. Without curiosity there can be no knowledge, no education, no exploration, no great questions. No book.

#3. feedback

The ability to process feedback allows us to continually learn from our mistakes and improve what we're doing.

With feedback you can get better and better at what you do. Without feedback there is no innovation, no progress, no research. No growth.

#4. empathy

Empathy, the ability to experience the world through the feelings of other people, is your biggest asset when writing for other people because it connects directly to their emotions.

One-day-old babies cry when they hear other babies crying. What's that all about? That is SuperPower number 4 switched on the day you are born.

With empathy you can see the world through the eyes of others. Without empathy we have no caring, no courage, no compassion. No love.

#5. imagination

And finally, imagination. The ability to distort the information coming into our senses and use it to dream great dreams or to put ourselves through hell.

With imagination we create, innovate and dream. Without imagination we have no art, no culture, no books, no music. No future.

When your SuperPowers are working in harmony, as they were on the day you were born, you can indeed start from nothing and learn as you go.

So, where better to start your exploration into writing a saleable self-help book than by helping yourself awaken and reignite your natural SuperPowers?

DAY 1 EXERCISE Awakening your SuperPowers

On a notepad recall three happy situations for each SuperPower listed on the following pages. Next, close your eyes for a minute or two and relive each situation. Vividly experience what you saw, heard and felt (include smell and taste if necessary) at the time._Note each experience in the boxes on the next two pages.

Three situations when I felt **Enthusiastic**

1. _____

2. _____

3. _____

Three situations when I experienced **Curiosity**

1. _____

2. _____

3. _____

Three situations when I processed **Feedback**

1. _____

2. _____

3. _____

Three situations when I experienced **Empathy**

1. _____

2. _____

3. _____

Three situations when I used my **Imagination**

1. _____

2. _____

3. _____

For each SuperPower, circle one memory from each of the five that you can relive most easily and vividly. Circle and underline the difficult ones. These are the SuperPowers you need to work hardest on next week as you reignite your SuperPowers.

That's it for today!

Reignite your SuperPowers

If you want to reignite your SuperPowers, it's easy. Just focus on one of them each day for a week. Don't tell anyone what you're doing. It will immediately deflate the energy and invalidate the exercise.

Monday - Get excited again like a child.

Tuesday - Ask questions, explore and talk to new people.

Wednesday - Figure out what you need to change to get what you want.

Thursday - Talk about the way things look, sound and feel.

Friday - Dream with no strings attached.

Saturday - Forget everything, go out and get involved, judge nothing, blame no one, and accept all reasonable invitations.

Sunday - Celebrate and rejoice.

That's it.

Chapter 3
Writing Madly

Maybe you've heard of a phenomenon called "automatic writing"? To many writers, it's a kind of zone, or flow, or voice they get themselves into where they write "like mad"—without stopping. Some people hail automatic writing as "channeling your higher self" or "accessing your unconscious mind."

Once you're in this "flow," you'll find that your knowledge, character, wisdom and memories from all the nooks and crannies of your heart and mind start to throw things at you as you write—at exactly the moment you need them. It's like being in the right place at the right time, or "the write place at the write time."

To ease you into the *Writing Madly* mindset, you'll spend just five minutes per question for the Day 2 exercise that's coming up.

Even if you think you've finished before the five minutes is up, keep writing. It's important for you to write for the full time period indicated in each exercise—it's part of the process. The golden rule is that you must not stop writing—even for a second—until your time is up. Your pen MUST always be moving or your fingers always typing.

Important tips:

- Pick a location where no one can disturb you or look over your shoulder to see what you're writing.
- Don't worry about what you write and don't allow your mind to edit or analyze the information while you're putting it down on paper.
- Give yourself permission to write the biggest load of rubbish you want. If you find yourself wandering off topic, bring yourself back.

- Push yourself until you break your "common sense" barrier.

When you've finished, come back and distill your answers in the box on the next page. Take a look over the following pages to see examples from my own books.

Rules for Writing Madly

- Your pen MUST always be moving or your fingers always typing—every second—until your time is up

- Don't edit or analyze the information while you're putting it down on paper

- Don't worry about what you write. Give yourself permission to write the biggest load of rubbish you want

- Push yourself beyond your "common sense" barrier

DAY 2 EXERCISE My expertise

On paper or your keyboard write one 5-MINUTE BURST PER QUESTION. If you finish before your five minutes is up, keep writing—even if it's just "I don't know what to write." It's part of the break-through process. **Summarize here then fold over the top corner of the page**.

1. **Why do I want to write a book?**

2. **What do I want to write about and why?**

3. **What knowledge do I have on this subject?**

4. **What is the unique benefit to the reader and why?**

Memorize your answers, then place your notes or printouts in your binder.

Summaries from How to Make
People Like You in 90 Seconds or Less

1. Why do I want to write a book?

I get excited when I meet people with potential and frustrated when I see they lack people skills.

2. What do I want to write about and why?

First impressions and how they lead to lasting relationships.

3. What knowledge do I have on this subject?

I was raised with good people skills and, as a fashion photographer, have spent twenty-five years connecting and communicating with dozens of new faces on a daily basis. I am a Master Practitioner of Neuro-Linguistic Programming.

4. What is the unique benefit to the reader and why?

I can show them, step by step, how to connect and communicate with all kinds of different people so they can have the confidence to make the most of their potential.

Summaries for my next book

(Distilled from my *Writing Madly* sessions)

1. Why do I want to write this book?

I see people getting old and acting old around me, and it drives me nuts because just because you're getting older doesn't mean you have to act old.

2. What do I want to write about and why?

How to live much longer than you expect to, and what's stopping you.

3. What knowledge do I have on this subject?

In researching my other books and doing in-depth interviews with thousands of people, I've made some observations about aging that shocked me.

4. What is the unique benefit to the reader and why?

They can live a long, healthy, meaningful life—if they want to—with no special diets, exercises or "magic potions."

Chapter 4
Never written before?
No problem!

I always wished I could write, but I never knew how. Then I got lucky, remember? I bumped into the editor of my local village weekly newspaper and she asked me to write that 300-word article for her paper.

Without thinking I said okay. But when she said she needed it by noon on Monday, I got the jitters.

On the drive back home I wondered, "Now what? I can't write. I've always wanted to—who hasn't? But I'm a photographer, not a writer."

Then I remembered something I learned twenty-five years ago.

Three little words

When I was in my early twenties, I sold advertising space for a woman's magazine with the largest circulation in Britain. I had the good fortune to work as assistant to a communications genius called Francis Xavier Muldoon. I have written extensively about my adventures with FXM in my books *How to Connect in Business in 90 Seconds or Less* and *Convince Them in 90 Seconds or Less,* and my readers love the stories.

Muldoon taught me a technique for writing short editorial pieces (about 300 words long) to promote a product. It went like this:

1. Ask yourself a question about the product.
2. Think of three individual words to link the product to the question.
3. Write a letter to an imaginary friend telling that person how great the product is, using each of the words in a separate paragraph.

He showed me how to "write like mad." His words.

"Just start writing off the top of your head. No hesitating. No stopping. No thinking. No editing. No coming up for air for ten minutes. Focus on tying those words to the product. When your ten minutes are up, take a break for a couple of minutes; then tidy it up, and we'll send it off to the editor. Editors work wonders."

If the average longhand writing speed is around twenty-five words per minute, you should end up with around two hundred and fifty words. The average typing speed comes in at around forty-five words per minute, so if you type, you'll have quite a lot more. An average page in this book (excluding chapter titles) is around one hundred and ninety words and, although today I type my books, I'm no faster than longhand speed.

That's just over a page in ten minutes. That's six pages an hour—or almost two hundred pages in thirty-three hours. Exactly the time it took me to write the first draft of this book. Naturally, a lot of words get chopped in the editing process.

It was amazing what came out of me in those sessions. Under that pressure, I remembered all sorts of odd things like ballet dancing and racing cars and donkey rides. It's amazing what your mind and your imagination throw up when they're in a hectic state. And that's the beauty of *Writing Madly*: you need content that is both rational and emotional to make it interesting and human.

Three hundred little words

When I got home, I thought about that article I'd just agreed to write about making people like you. I knew I had to focus on just one aspect, so I chose eye contact.

"Warmth, words and trust" were the three words that popped into my mind. So I wrote for ten minutes. I wrote about how eyes can project warmth or hostility or cruelty, how your words go where your eyes go and how eye contact sends an unconscious signal that trust is in the air. I had also put down a few incomplete thoughts that I went back to and finished off. Then I tidied it all up, rearranged a couple of things and dropped it off at the newspaper office.

The next week, the editor asked me for another piece. So I wrote three hundred words about personal space. This time, my instant three words were: social, personal and private.

Those two three-hundred-word articles became the basis for two chapters in my first book. And two chapters are enough to show a publisher whether or not you can write. All I had to do next was come up with nine more chapters.

The pajama game

By this time, I was doing a couple of speaking engagements a month, and people were starting to ask if I had a book. I'd say no and recommend other people's books. It was about time I got serious about writing my own.

I made a deal with myself. I couldn't get dressed each day until I'd written 1,500 words. I certainly wasn't a writer, but I asked myself, "How hard could it be? Look at all the people who write!" And besides, I had a computer, I could write and speak English, I had a sense of humor and I was now passionate about the subject.

But it didn't help. I'd spend hours at a stretch trying to come up with a fully formed chapter. That might work for the professionals, but it wasn't working for me.

Then I heard Muldoon's voice over my shoulder. "Just dash it off in ten-minute bursts."

So I did. At the end of my first burst, I was so buzzed I did another one, then another until I'd done 1,500 words. I was *Writing Madly*, and it worked.

Then I heard Muldoon again. "Send it off to the editor. Editors work wonders."

What exactly do editors do?

Editors are the invisible heroes of the publishing world. There are several kinds of editors, but these are the main ones you need to know about:

Acquisitions editor: Acquires manuscripts for the publishing house.

Developmental editor: Usually works in-house for a publisher. Works with a writer to plan the book's structure and develop an outline, and may coach the writer chapter by chapter. Your publisher may assign a developmental editor to your project.

Substantive or structural editor: May work in-house or freelance. Works on the big-picture issues: content, structure, flow, tone, voice (in fiction: plot, characters, chronology and more). May first get involved after the first draft is completed and the writer wants objective feedback to improve the book, or advice on some problematic aspects of the book.

Copy editor: May work in-house or freelance. After the big-picture issues have been sorted out, this editor works on grammar, spelling, punctuation and style issues (what gets capitalized, what gets italicized, how to treat numbers, and much more). Also checks facts. The goals of copy editing, summed up in the four Cs, are to make your writing:

1. **clear**

2. **correct**

3. **consistent**

4. **concise**

Some editors specialize in one of the above types of editing; but some can, and will, do it all. Many, like my editor Marie Lynn, find their work often turns into coaching—that is, helping writers develop their skills rather than just fixing their mistakes.

If editors are invisible, how do I find one?

To find an editor, ask other writers, search the Web, or check out professional associations such as www.editors.ca, where you can search by skill, subject matter and more. Often you can ask for a sample edit of a couple of pages, but this won't tell you much about the editor's structural skills. For that, you ask for testimonials or references from other writers they've worked with.

And finally, if you have a great concept and lots of expertise—and money—but you've discovered while working your way through this book that writing just isn't your cup of tea, you can always hire a ghostwriter. You wouldn't be the first! And you'll still end up with a book that packages *your* ideas and *your* expertise.

A perfect ten

The difference between people who accomplish a lot and those who don't is **focus**. Ten minutes of *Writing Madly* is a realistic amount of time to hold on to your focus while at the same time being able to hold off unwanted interruptions. It's also a slice of time where the end is always in sight. This creates energy, and with energy comes excitement. Excitement plus focus can equal a flood of inspired writing.

Ten minutes is usually enough to get you well into the writing zone. When you run out of things to write before your time is up, keep writing. Write whatever comes into your head, even if it's just "I've run out of things to say and I don't know where to go from here but ..." No stopping, not for a second.

As you write in this way, you'll find your subconscious mind will unpack and access all kinds of knowledge you've accumulated over the years, which you'll need to build your book.

On day three you'll write madly to access your visceral, gut emotions and limits, on day four you'll write normally to perform due diligence on your idea, then it's back to *Writing Madly* again on day five to brainstorm and finesse your book idea.

After that on to writing your ten Key Chapters.

DAY 3 EXERCISE My passions

One 10-MINUTE BURST PER QUESTION. Even if you think you're done in five seconds, keep going for the full ten minutes. **Summarize below.**

1. What are three things that turn you on and make time stand still, and why?

a)

b)

c)

2. What are three things that have driven you mad since you were a child, and why?

a)

b)

c)

3. What are three things that come easily for you, but not necessarily for everyone else?

a)

b)

c)

Place your notes or printouts in your binder.

Chapter 5
Due diligence

Preliminary research

In my writing workshops, I often ask students, "Who is the biggest expert in the world on your topic?"

Ninety percent of the time, they don't know.

I say, "You should know, because they're your competition."

Here are a few important questions to answer before you write your book. *Go online, visit bookstores, ask around and look for the answers. Write them down, and put your notes in the folder.*

DAY 4 EXERCISE   Due diligence

NORMAL SPEED AS LONG AS YOU NEED

1. Who is the biggest expert in the world, the country and my community on my particular topic?

a) World

b) Country

c) Community

2. Has my book already been written by someone else?

Make sure your book hasn't already been written. If it has, figure out how to make your book different, better and more relevant. Don't be put off if someone has beaten you to it. When I wrote my first book, *How to Make People Like You in 90 Seconds or Less*, I had to find a way to surpass one of the best-selling books of all time, Dale Carnegie's classic *How to Win Friends and Influence People*. A self-help book is first and foremost an invention, so you have to be a creative inventor.

3. Which three main titles am I competing against?

Search your title or concept online and see what sites come up. See which titles get the most stars on Amazon and GoodReads, which ones are *NY Times* best sellers, or which have the biggest sales.

a)

b)

c)

4. Who's going to sell my book?

When you self-publish, your portion of the profits go to you after paying all the expenses such as printing, editing, designers, photographers, publicists, book tour, travel, consignment fees, commissions and so on.

Most conventional publishers take care of all these expenses and then pay between 6% and 12% of the retail price in royalties to you, and from that you'll probably hand over 15% to your agent—for life. Self-publishing and e-publishing offer far better royalty rates; however, a conventional publisher may well take your book to an event like the Frankfurt Book Fair and sell off the foreign rights. This is huge. Think of three ways you can sell your books.

a)

b)

c)

5. Who's going to buy my book?

The more tightly you can define your market, the more accurately you can target it.

There are hundreds of books about baking cakes. But one day, Anne Byrn wrote *The Cake Mix Doctor*—a book with a simple twist. By doctoring up packaged cake mix with just the right extras—a touch of sweet butter here, cocoa powder there, or a dash of poppy seeds and vanilla yogurt—she produced a series of foolproof, best-selling books that transformed the art of home baking in America.

a)

b)

c)

Chapter 6
Someone gets brutally killed!

.

I once saw the chairman of a Fortune 500 company come on stage to address an audience wearing a blindfold to hook the audience's attention. She went on to point out the organization had lost its way, and presented her solutions. I watched another CEO pretend he couldn't pull his hands out of his pockets for thirty seconds to hook the audience's attention and point out the need for budget restraints. Newspapers use shocking headlines to hook your attention and make a point. Public speakers kick off their talks with provocative quotations to hook your attention and make a point. Advertisers tease you with stunning statistics, and "Law and Order" always shows someone getting brutally killed in the first ninety seconds of the show for the very same reason.

What do all these things have in common? They're emotional hooks for rational points. Grabbing your attention, holding your interest and offering solutions.

Hooks and Points

A killer title is a crucial hook. Even if it's only a working title, a great self-help title **must include or imply a benefit**. Remember, a benefit is anything that makes your reader's life better, faster, cheaper, happier, tastier and so on. For example:

What To Expect When You're Expecting

Think and Grow Rich

The Cake Mix Doctor

How to Make People Like You in 90 Seconds or Less

The Barbecue Bible

Subtle might work in literary fiction, but it never works in self-help book titles unless you're famous. You need your own emotional "hook" and rational "point."

- The "hook" gets the audience's **attention** and holds their **interest**.
- The "point" tells the audience what the book is all about and, in doing so, incites a **desire** that gets them to take **action**.

This formula—Attention, Interest, Desire, Action—is at the heart of all successful communication—be it a book, a chapter or a speech.

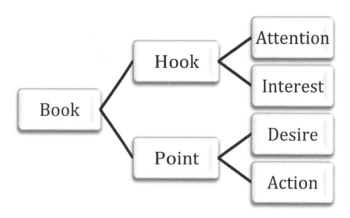

The golden rule for any presentation, be it a movie, a story, a business presentation or a self-help book, is this: "no point, no presentation."

Nothing exasperates an audience more than not knowing *why* they are watching a movie, listening to a speech or reading a book. From the moment they open your book, your audience is thinking, "Why am I reading this, and what's in it for me?" Or, "What's the point of this book?" Just like you were doing at the start of this book.

The **hook** is *how to write a saleable book in ten-minute bursts of madness.* If it doesn't grab your attention and pique your interest, it has failed.

The **point** of the book is: *when you lay down your entire book from beginning to end in quick painless chunks, finishing, polishing and promoting is ten times easier.*

What's the point of your book?

The real point of your self-help book may not necessarily be what you think it is.

Take my friend, Charlie. He might say, "My book is about building houses, and my point is that I can help you build a better, energy-efficient house." But that's not really a point.

A point should involve **cause** and **effect**. "**When** you do this...**then** that will happen." "**When** people like you, **then** they see the best in you." For example, what was the point of *Lord of the Rings*? **When** two little guys throw a ring into a volcano, **then** the world will be saved.

So Charlie needs to think about his book this way: "The point is, when you plan your house the way I'm going to show you, when you build a foundation the way I'm going to show you, and when you frame, wire, plumb, etc., the way I'm going to show you [**cause**], then you will have a superior and energy-efficient house [**effect**]."

DAY 5 EXERCISE Hooks and points

Take TEN MINUTES of *Writing Madly* for each question. Even if you think you're done in five seconds, keep going for the full ten minutes. **Summarize below then fold over the top corner of the page.**

1. **What's the hook of my book?**

2. **What's the point of my book?**

3. **What's my fresh take that might interest a publisher?**

4. **What's my killer title?**

My actual notes from How to Make People Like You in 90 Seconds or Less

(Distilled from my *Writing Madly* sessions)

1. What's my **hook**?

You can connect with all types of people in 90 seconds or less and enjoy it.

2. What's my **fresh take** that might interest a publisher?

The audacity of the time element.

3. What's the **point** of my book?

When you do certain things in a certain order, people will trust, like and feel comfortable with you.

4. What's my **killer title**?

How to Make People Like You in 90 Seconds or Less

Actual notes for my next book

(Distilled from my *Writing Madly* sessions)

1.   What's my **hook**?

How to Survive to a Hundred and Five

2.   What's my **fresh take** that might interest a publisher?

You can live a long, healthy, meaningful life with no special diets, exercises or "magic potions."

3.   What's the **point** of my book?

Self-talk, lifestyle, your postal code and your unwillingness to take risks have more effect on your longevity than diet and exercise.

4.   What's my **killer title**?

How to Survive to a Hundred and Five

your best testimonial

your
"killer"
title

your unique benefit

your name
your credentials

A Saleable Self-Help/ How-to cover has a killer title with a unique benefit for a definable market, can be read from 15ft away and appeals instantly to a reviewer.

A killer title:

- tells readers what the book is about
- promises a reward
- states something provocative
- creates curiosity
- is catchy and easy to remember
- works well as a headline in a magazine article, a blog or a TV segment
- tells readers who you are and who says you're great

Credentials and credibility

If there's one place that aspiring self-help authors make or break it, it's in the credibility and trustworthiness department.

Credentials demonstrate your trustworthiness as an expert, and they come in many forms: a document or certificate proving your professional qualification—like a lawyer, professor or doctor might have. Maybe you have your own radio or TV show or you're a well-respected blogger, newscaster, sports personality, celebrity or record holder.

Your credibility comes from third-party endorsements, and the bigger the better. It doesn't mean much if your Uncle Oscar and the lady at the 7-Eleven think you're fabulous. You need the guy on *Breakfast Television* or the *National Morning Newspaper* or the president of Campbell's soup to say you're great.

If you want people to buy your book, you need to start collecting, compiling and earning your credentials today in order to build your credibility.

You'll find more about this on page 131.

PART TWO: PRODUCING

The exercises in this section are designed to help you, the author, lead your reader safely and enjoyably across an imaginary stream. On the near bank they are hungry to share your expertise. By the time you reach the far bank together they will have absorbed and tested your wisdom.

In less than an hour a day, for the next ten days, you will write ten Key Chapters (KC). These Key Chapters form the mainstay of your self-help book. The exercises are designed to bypass that little voice inside you that says "you can't say that," and let your true potential come out and lay itself on the page.

Keep your book to yourself until you complete your second draft. When working with your editor, you know what you want to say, and it's your editor's job to help you to say it in the clearest and most concise way. You work as a team to produce the best book possible. But if you let others see your work before it is ready, you will get all kinds of opinions, and you'll begin to doubt yourself and your writing.

Each Key Chapter is like a stepping stone with a Shish-Kebab waiting on it.

An emotional three-part opening including the point, the who, where, when, why, what and how.

KC1

KC2

KC3

KC4

KC5

KC6

KC7

KC8

KC9

An emotional two-part close.

KC10

This is how we made it. Where do we go from here?

Chapter 7
Crossing the stream

Writing a self-help book is kind of like guiding your reader across a fast-flowing stream on a series of stepping stones. The stream is the problem, dilemma or ambition, the stepping stones are the path to a solution and the flow of the river mirrors your involvement and enjoyment. Sometimes you have to go ahead of your reader to guide them, at other times you go behind in case they drop something and occasionally, you take their hand to make sure they don't slip. Eight stepping stones are usually sufficient. On each stone you find a Shish-

Kebab to share with your reader—that's a metaphor for the contents of your chapter. You'll learn all about Shish-Kebabs later in this chapter.

You start your journey together on the near bank in Key Chapter one (KC1), step onto the different stones and make your way across the stream in Key Chapter 2 through 9, and end your book, in the final Key Chapter (KC10), when you step onto the opposite bank. That makes ten chapters in all.

At the start, standing at the river's edge, you set up your book with an emotional, three part opening. This includes the point of your book, along with the who, the where, the when, the why and the how.

Being the stream

In your minds eye, picture a fast-flowing stream running through a forest. The water is clear, cool and fresh. The canopy above offers you shade and safety. Both banks are green and mossy giving way to rocks and then a series of eight stepping stones that form a path to the far bank. With your eyes closed look around and up and down and see what you can see. The shapes, the colors, the movements. Listen carefully and hear what you can hear—not just the water but perhaps a bird, the wind in the canopy above. Feel what you can feel. Perhaps the soft moss beneath your feet, a fine spray from the stream or the breeze in your clothing. What can you smell? What can you taste? This is your stream, in your forest. Take as long as you like to become one with your stream.

Picture yourself guiding your reader across the stream to the far bank. Understand you can take nothing for granted. You must show, not tell, your reader what the steps are, what's coming up, what to look out for. You can show them shortcuts and how to avoid risks but, at all times, they must feel they can trust you, your reasoning makes sense and they are moved by you.

DAY 6 EXERCISE A letter to a friend of a friend

You are going to write a letter to A FRIEND OF A FRIEND telling them all about your book. <u>The person you are writing to doesn't know you.</u>

Writing to a friend of a friend sharpens your focus and improves the quality of your writing.

Take FIFTEEN MINUTES to roughly outline all three parts.

The first part must include:

- A statistic about your topic
- Impressive information about who you are and why they should trust you
- Why you are moved to write the book
- Why your book is different from all the others

The second part must include:

- Who, specifically, is your ultimate reader
- A brief, true story, relevant to why you are writing the book
- What is the unique benefit to the reader
- Why the reader would pick up your book

The third part must include:

- What's coming up in the book
- What's your promise to your reader
- How are you going to keep your promise
- Another brief, true story relevant to writing the book

When you are ready, spend TEN MINUTES of Writing Madly for each of these three parts. Make your words warm and friendly and write in a voice any eight year old child could understand.

Steak and sizzle

Eighty percent of the time people make their decisions based on their emotions, even if they think they're being rational. In Marketing 101 we ask, "Does a man buy a drill because he wants to buy a drill, or does he buy it because he wants to drill a hole?" "Or does he buy it because he wants to drill a hole to hang a picture of his family on the wall so he can feel good?" Just about everything we do can be traced to making us feel good.

If you want to write a self-help book that sells, it can't just be a dull manual; it has to appeal to the senses. Your book needs to be more exciting and captivating than the competition's book. If *you're* not excited and feeling good about every chapter, your audience isn't going to be excited and feel good either—and they will soon put your book aside.

A simple way to let your excitement shine through is to think of each key chapter as a shish kebab. Again, you're using a hook and a point, but this time adding some "steak" and some "sizzle." In this context, *steak* is the hard facts, instructions and exercises your readers need in order to follow the steps you are giving them. The *sizzle* can be an engaging anecdote—a short, amusing or interesting story about a real incident or person—to illustrate your *point* and keep your reader entertained.

Your first draft will comprise of ten Key Chapters. Each one answers a question and begins with a title, a hook and a point. It is divided into three sections, each of which begins with a **heading**. Each section covers a topic that relates to the point of the chapter.

Each of the three sections will be further divided into three smaller parts. Each of these smaller parts begins with a **subheading**.

Let's say you're writing a book about renovating your dream house. You have decided to write a chapter that answers this important question:

"What are the dangers of taking shortcuts?"

To answer this question, you decide your answer will be divided into these three sections:

1. the probability you'll fail a building inspection

2. the fact that shortcuts are frequently more expensive in the long run and

3. the dangers you'll likely face in the future

So in this example, you decide that "Inspectors! Necessary Evils?" is your first heading. "What's All that Black Stuff on the Rafters?" is the second heading, and "See You in Court" is the third.

For each of these headings you now need to come up with three factual examples to support your discussions, tips and techniques, and give each one a subheading. (See the example on page 81.)

Headings and subheadings are not set in stone. You can change them or have more or fewer, as you wish. They may well disappear or be replaced later in the editing or rewriting process.

These headings and subheadings are your *steak*—your hard facts and data. They're all good—but they lack sizzle—there's no saleability wow factor. To add some *sizzle* to your *steak,* you must draw on your past experiences and tell one or two true stories or anecdotes. These can be placed anywhere in the chapter. Later, in the chapter on STORYspeak, you'll find simple techniques to bring your anecdotes and stories alive.

Perhaps you know about a guy who skipped a few steps in his kitchen renovation, only to have the upper kitchen cupboards collapse on top of the Thanksgiving dinner when he was entertaining his boss and his boss's entire family.

Or, you read somewhere about a woman who refused to let the building inspector look in her attic because there had been an electrical fire up there two years ago and she had lied about it. Now the insurance company is refusing to cover the cost of replacing the roof shingles that rotted prematurely.

Here's how a completed Key Chapter outline looks.

Key Chapter – The Dangers of Taking Shortcuts	
Question – *What are the dangers of taking shortcuts?*	
Hook – *You can't fool a home inspector, but that doesn't stop people from trying.*	
Point – *If you're going to make a quick fix, think it through thoroughly ahead of time.*	

Heading	**Subheading**
Inspectors! Necessary evils?	1. Their roles 2. Credentials 3. Powers
What's all that black stuff on the rafters?	1. The clues 2. Ignorance, liars and cheats 3. Start over!
See you in court	1. Insurance horror stories 2. The sale fell through 3. Your property ends here

DAY 7 EXERCISE #1 Key Chapter outline

You are a passionate citizen writing about life in your town or city. Using public transport, grocery shopping and healthcare as your headings, fill in all the rest—the title, question, hook, point and subheading from your imagination. (See Appendix for examples.)

Key Chapter title –	
Question –	
Hook –	
Point –	
Heading	**Subheading**
Public Transport	1. 2. 3.
Grocery Shopping	1. 2. 3.
Healthcare	1. 2. 3.

DAY 7 EXERCISE #2 Key Chapter outline

You are a teenager, and you want to teach people in your neighborhood how to give back to the community. Using donating, green space and hunger as your headings, fill in the title, question, hook, point and subheadings from your own imagination.

Key Chapter title –	
Question –	
Hook –	
Point –	
Heading	**Subheading**
Donating	1. 2. 3.
Green Space	1. 2. 3.
Hunger	1. 2. 3.

Ideas for Key Chapters

Use this box to jot down ideas for Key Chapters that are fundamental to your book.

Chapter 8
It's time to write
a book

Over the next ten days you're going to write a complete first draft, starting with your emotional opening chapter, followed by eight more chapters containing a series of rational steps and rounding out with an emotional closing chapter that looks at where you've come from and where you're going from here. That means you have to write a total of nine Key Chapters to complete your first draft.

"Why only nine? Nick, surely you have miscalculated. That should be ten chapters and not nine!"

No, my math is correct because you have already written your emotional opening chapter.

Remember the three-part letter to a friend of a friend? That letter has all the elements you need to kick your book off to a flying start. Of course it must be rewritten and polished to fully connect, get leverage and buy-in, but that will come later.

Right now, you are about to guide your reader on to the first of the eight stepping stones. This is where your expertise takes over. Only you know what comes first. If you're writing a book about stepping out of your comfort zone to find new opportunities, it might mean looking at how you got where you are. If it's a book about becoming an internet millionaire you might look at the history of millionaires. Whatever your topic, this is where your expertise takes over. You are the expert now and you have to come up with eight steps to take your reader from an amateur to an authority. When you feel the urge to combine or add more chapters, save it for your second draft.

Each daily exercise will take about sixty minutes, including the writing.

1. Take FIFTEEN MINUTES to fill in the entire outline: i.e. the chapter title, the question the chap-

ter answers, the headings and the subheadings. If you have trouble coming up with the hook and the point don't worry: these elements will become clear in the rewriting process.

2. Then TEN MINUTES writing about each section: i.e. A heading and it's three subheadings

a. TEN MINUTES for Public Transport

b. TEN MINUTES for Grocery Shopping

c. TEN MINUTES for Healthcare

	Key Chapter title – Question – Hook – Point –	
Minutes	**Heading**	**Subheading**
10	Public Transport	1. Safety 2. Cost 3. Options
10	Grocery Shopping	1. Farm fresh 2. Entertaining 3. Ethnic
10	Healthcare	1. Doctors 2. Hospitals 3. Emergency

DAYS 8 and 9 EXERCISES

Key Chapter 2 –
Question –
Hook –
Point –

Heading	Subheading
1.	1. 2. 3.
2.	1. 2. 3.
3.	1. 2. 3.

Key Chapter 3 –
Question –
Hook –
Point –

Heading	Subheading
1.	1. 2. 3.
2.	1. 2. 3.
3.	1. 2. 3.

Find your voice

Besides helping make your book more exciting and entertaining, *Writing Madly* will give you access to your "voice."

A writer's voice is his or her individual writing style. One author may have a voice that is enthusiastic and upbeat, while another may have a cheeky voice bordering on sarcastic. Your voice may be anything from humorous to heartfelt, or savvy to serious, and it can help make your writing unique. It embodies your attitude and personality and makes your book human. Your voice should be appropriate to the subject matter. You don't want a joking voice for a book on grief counseling, or a heavy academic voice for a book on how to be a stand-up comedian.

As you get up to speed with *Writing Madly*, you'll be able to bulldoze your conscious mind aside and open up the unlimited power of your subconscious. When this happens, you'll access a voice inside that throws words and ideas up to you just when you need them. Eventually your own individual writer's voice will start to emerge on the page so that your reader feels you are really speaking directly to him or her.

DAYS 10 and 11 EXERCISES	
Key Chapter 4 – **Question –** **Hook –** **Point –**	
Heading	**Subheading**
1.	1. 2. 3.
2.	1. 2. 3.
3.	1. 2. 3.
Key Chapter 5 – **Question –** **Hook –** **Point –**	
Heading	**Subheading**
1.	1. 2. 3.
2.	1. 2. 3.
3.	1. 2. 3.

DAYS 12 and 13 EXERCISES	
Key Chapter 6 – **Question –** **Hook –** **Point –**	
Heading	**Subheading**
1.	1. 2. 3.
2.	1. 2. 3.
3.	1. 2. 3.
Key Chapter 7 – **Question –** **Hook –** **Point –**	
Heading	**Subheading**
1.	1. 2. 3.
2.	1. 2. 3.
3.	1. 2. 3.

DAYS 14 and 15 EXERCISES

Key Chapter 8 –
Question –
Hook –
Point –

Heading	Subheading
1.	1. 2. 3.
2.	1. 2. 3.
3.	1. 2. 3.

Key Chapter 9 –
Question –
Hook –
Point –

Heading	Subheading
1.	1. 2. 3.
2.	1. 2. 3.
3.	1. 2. 3.

DAY 16 EXERCISE Key Chapter 10

Write a letter to the friend, whose friend you guided across the stream. Tell him, or her about your journey. This letter will form the base of your emotional close.

Part 1. TEN MINUTES

Begin with a recap. Talk about the obstacles overcome, the techniques learned, the people encountered, the exercises practiced etc. You are the expert. You, the author, know where you went and what you did.

Part 2. TEN MINUTES

Have a heart to heart with your reader about where to go from here. You can't just leave your reader in the lurch. They are on the far bank now and want to know their options. Be proud of your progress together, have a laugh, tell a story, boost their confidence and give them a next step.

Congratulations!

You have written content for ten Key Chapters. You've passed your first milestone and it's time for a change of pace.

Tomorrow you are going to take your *Writing Madly* sessions from days 6, 8, 9, 10, 11, 12, 13, 15, 15 and 16 and convert them into a rough first draft. Then you'll create your first table of contents.

To do this you'll need all your notes and your ten Key Chapters in electronic form. If they're already on your computer, that's great. If not, please transcribe them. Take a few minutes to correct typos and tie up any obvious loose ends.

Chapter 9
Table of
contents

Since I started my writing career, I've worked my way through most of the writing software programs available, but I always come back to Microsoft Word. If you have your own favorite writing program, by all means use it. Let me share how Word works for me.

I write as WYSIWYG (What You See Is What You Get) as I possibly can because it helps me flow.

I format my pages at 5" x 7" facing and use a 22" monitor. This allows me to see up to twenty-four (more or less) pages at a time for planning. Most of the time, I write with a double page spread on my screen—as if I were reading the book. It's a little more difficult on my laptop, but it still works.

I use the Styles function and set the *Body* of my books in 12 point Garamond. I set the *Chapter Titles* in 40 point bold Calibri, the *Headings* in 20 point bold Calibri and the *Exercises* in 12 point bold Garamond. I set the Table of Contents to automatically generate from the last three styles.

however . . .

What an agent, publisher or editor wants to receive from you is a plain document, preferably in Microsoft Word, double spaced, using 12 point Times New Roman font and justified left only. At most, you can bold your chapter titles and subheadings, but don't get distracted from writing by playing around with different fonts, layouts, colors, page sizes and so on. My editors prefer a one inch margin of the left and two inches on the right.

If you want certain material to go into a box, or sidebar, as they're known—like a checklist or some additional information that doesn't easily fit into your various chapter sections—don't fiddle around creating boxes with fancy borders. Just format like this:

[BEGIN SIDEBAR]

Additional Information

This is a sidebar containing information that some readers may find useful but which doesn't easily fit into my chapter sections.

Put more info, or your list, here and then at the end, type the following:

[END SIDEBAR]

but anyway . . .

DAY 17 EXERCISE Creating a table of contents

Take all the time you need.

Set the Styles that work for you on your own word processor—feel free to use mine for the time being if you wish. I made my chapter titles huge because I like them that way. You can set your own to suit your book. Obviously, if you're writing a book on herbal teas from your own garden, you might choose a smaller, more sensible and less jarring font!

You probably wrote your chapter topics out of sequence, so arrange your binder in an order that makes sense and flows logically.

1. Rearrange your *Writing Madly* sessions in your computer to follow the same order as your .
2. Put the title of your book on the first page along with your name, contact details and a copyright symbol with the date. Write "First Draft" in the header and insert © along with the year and your name in the footer.
3. Assign your headings and subheadings throughout each chapter to highlight important points, exercises or tasks. Feel free to create new ones if they work better.
4. Assign a Style to each.
5. Place your cursor at the top of page 3, type "Contents" and hit return.
6. Insert your Table of Contents right here.
7. Print your first draft and set it aside for tomorrow.

That's it for today.

DAY 18 EXERCISE Read your first printed draft.

Feel free to re-arrange, split, merge or create new chapters. If you do, update your Table of Contents and reprint your first draft.

Chapter 10
Bringing my
Book Alive

For the next 30 days you are going to spend three days per chapter fleshing out your Writing Madly sessions. If you have 10 chapters that's 30 days of writing. If you have more (or less) chapters you must adjust your time accordingly with three days per chapter. Bear in mind that your words do have to eventually end up in electronic form so they can be edited.

Elaborate on your ideas, rearrange them, focus your thoughts, add to your details, build your steps and reinforce your techniques. At this point don't worry about including stories and exercises—that will come later.

Aim for between 500 and 750 words a day. At 250 words per finished page that comes in at around 2 to 3 finished pages a day. Ernest Hemingway wrote around 500 finished words a day, Stephen King comes in at around 1500 and JK Rowling confesses, "I pretty much sit down and keep going until I'm too exhausted to continue. Some days, I can do a very, very, very hard day's work and not write a word, just revising, or I'd just scribble a few words." If you take the number of words in Harry Potter and the Chamber of Secrets (85,141) and divide it by the number of days she took to write the book (368 days) you'll find Ms. Rowling averaged 231 words a day.

Many Self-Help/How-to writers come in between 750 and 1,250 words a day. The process is a bit like panning for gold. The more stuff you put in the pan, the more nuggets you'll find.

Lots of today's writers start early in the day, around 5 or 6 am, and are finished by 8 or 9 am. If you have a full time job this might be the schedule for you. Either that, or late at night.

As you bring your book alive be sure to mark your progress on the next page. Your goal is to do a complete pass of your book, so stick with the schedule and initial each box as you go. A common fault among beginners is they get hooked on polishing their first 10 pages over and over again and never get around to bringing the rest of their book alive. There'll be plenty of time for polishing later.

DAYS 19 THROUGH 48 EXERCISES – Bringing My Book Alive

My Progress

Chapters	1	2	3	4	5	6	7	8	9	10
Day 1										
Day 2										
Day 3										

At the end of Day 48, update your Table of Contents, write "second draft" in your header and print your manuscript.

Tomorrow is Day 49 and time to move your writing skills up to the next level with STORYspeak.

PART THREE: POLISHING

"*The research is the easiest. The outline is the most fun. The first draft is the hardest, because every word of the outline has to be fleshed out. The rewrite is very satisfying.*"

Ken Follett

Chapter 11
STORYspeak-it

Facts and figures fade fast, but once upon a time lasts forever.

We've all heard that a picture is worth a thousand words. And it is. Just try to describe an elephant or a sunset or a barbecue, and you'll find you can do it more effectively and quickly by showing a picture.

I have three great tools to share with you that will give your words the power of pictures. They are simple ways for creating memorable, mental images of what you want to communicate to other people—be they ideas, values, motivation, knowledge or emotions.

I call these tools STORYspeak, and they are:

1. writing in color
2. shish kebabs (which we already covered)
3. stepping stones

The genius of all great self-help writers lies in their ability to these tools to make things more interesting, to captivate, to explain and to inspire their readers.

Parables, fables, storytelling and anecdotes are some of the oldest and most powerful communication tools we have. We all love a good story. It appeals to the senses and fires up the imagination, which in turn cranks up your emotions. Metaphors and stories make understanding easier, quicker and richer because the right side of the brain likes to deal in pictures or stories and can make quick associations.

This is precisely what STORYspeak is all about: getting your point across quickly with memorable mental images, images that connect with the imagination.

All writing is enhanced by painting word pictures of your experiences for other people. This is where the SuperPowers of curiosity, empathy and imagination are triggered in you and your reader. The more vividly and simply you can describe these experiences, the more emotions you'll arouse in your reader. People will find your book to be more interesting and will be more likely to understand your message.

The next four days of exercises are designed to help you learn STORYspeak. The exercises will not form part of your book so they don't need to be transcribed onto your computer: they are simply to help you learn in a natural way at an easy pace.

Make sure your skills build from exercise to exercise by increasing your use of the way things look, sound, feel, smell and even taste.

Write out your answers in long-hand. The purpose here is to create a body-mind-time connection.

Have fun and see if you can incorporate "Talking in Color" into your daily routines.

DAY 49 EXERCISE #1 Thinking in Color

Before you can write in color, you need to practice thinking in color. Close your eyes and imagine you're at a busy train station. Your train was cancelled and now you, and lots of other people, have to wait an hour before the next train. Write down everything you can see, hear, touch, taste and smell. Summarize here.

SEE	HEAR	TOUCH	TASTE	SMELL

When you have made your list, take thirty seconds to describe to yourself out loud and in sharp detail what you see, then take another thirty seconds to do the same for what you hear, then what you feel (physical sensations), smell and taste. Notice which of the senses came most easily and which was the most difficult? Pay extra attention to the difficult ones and work hard at incorporating them into your stories—your readers will thank you.

Writing in color

Here's a black-and-white description of an everyday event: *We stood in line for the bus for more than twenty minutes. I was so fed up!*

Here's the same event described "in color": *I was helpless and impotent standing there in silence among all those people. I peeled back my glove and squinted at my watch.*

"I don't have time for this!" I complained to myself.

The rain stopped, water ran down my neck and I tightened my collar. I was miserable. The lights of the buildings shimmered like candles in the puddles, and the hot dog vendor behind me cursed. Two minutes earlier the smell of his fried onions made me......

DAY 49 EXERCISE #2 Writing in Color

With this example as your guide, write a description of your last commute to work "in black and white." 50 WORDS

Next, write a description of that same commute "in color." You can use past or present tense. 250-500 WORDS

DAY 49 EXERCISE #3 The story of my life

Write in color topic here is: The Story of My Life. **Be sure to include sensory details.** 500 WORDS

When you've finished, you're going to play editor and reduce it all into "the thirty-second story of my life." That means you can read it out loud, in your normal voice, in thirty seconds. 50-100 WORDS.

You're well on your way to being a colorful writer. Are you noticing how your SuperPowers of enthusiasm, curiosity, feedback, empathy and imagination are coming into play here and working along with you?

Stories add sizzle

Stories are to the human heart what food is to the body. Advertisers polish them, marketers spread them, lawyers bend them, religions exalt them and authors thrive off of them. We watch them unfold on the screen, read them in books and, when we can't find one handy, we make them up. And no wonder. We are natural-born storytellers—it's in our genes.

DAY 50 EXERCISE #1 A good decision I made

Write 250-500 WORDS about a good decision you made in your personal life. Use this template.

Hook – There I was (who/where/when) . . .

when suddenly (describe what happened) . . .

so then (I) . . .

And now (the resolution) . . .

Point/Moral of the story . . .

Note: This exercise does not need to be transcribed later.

A cast of characters

Telling stories via characters and writing in the third person is by far the most compelling way to spice up your book. Even if you have five true stories about yourself, move four of them into the third person and make them about someone else. Feel free to change the names, location, age, season and gender. Unless you want to seriously limit your saleability be sure to cast your characters from a variety of ethnic backgrounds with suitable names to match.

DAY 50 EXERCISE #2 A bad decision she made

In this exercise you are going to Write in Color about a bad decision you made in your personal life using the same template. 500 WORDS

Except this time you are going to <u>write it in the third person.</u> If you are a man, make your character a woman. If you are a woman, write it as a man.

Hook – There he/she was (who/where/when) . . .

when suddenly (describe what happened) . . .

so then . . .

And now (the resolution) . . .

Point/Moral of the story . . .

Note: This exercise does not need to be transcribed later.

More stepping stones

Telling a story is also like crossing a fast-flowing stream on stepping stones. The stream is the problem or dilemma, and the stones are the path to a solution. Again, ten stones are usually sufficient. You start the story on one bank, step onto the different stones on the way across the stream, and begin your close when you step onto the opposite bank.

At the start, standing at the river's edge, you set up the story by declaring your hook and stating your point. It's here that you introduce the character/s (the who), the location (the where), and the time (the when).

Say you're writing a book titled *Romance Rehab* and you're writing a chapter called "Reliving your Hippie Years." One of your headings is "travel agents," and you're making the point that in today's world it's best to use an agent for complex trips.

Instead of writing yet another first-hand story about your own experiences, you decide to move your adventures into the third person to make it more interesting. You begin with the who, the where, the when, the point and the problem.

So, instead of starting with, "Last summer I..." you write:

Last summer, my neighbor Sammy decided he'd use the money he stood to save by installing his brand-new kitchen himself to take his wife for an exotic holiday to South America. Little did Sammy know that online booking was not the way to go.

Stepping onto the first stone, you explain the problem, dilemma or predicament. *The problem was that Sammy had never so much as changed a light bulb before . . . .*

Moving out onto the second stone in the middle of the fast-flowing stream, you describe some of the problems and Sammy's failed attempts at resolving them, before leaping onto the last stone and revealing the successful solution.

As you step onto the far bank, you deliver your emotional "close" and state your point again. At this time you can invite your listeners to look to the future and imagine themselves in the same situation. Using what they learned from this story, they can resolve the problem. All you need to write is: "Just imagine . . . " or "The next time you are faced with . . . "

DAY 51 EXERCISE A third person story

Imagine your character fell asleep on the last bus home listening to music and missed his, or her, stop. Now, at the end of the line, with a dead phone battery your character has to get home. Begin by filling out the ten steps below.

1) The point

2) The who

3) The where

4) The when

5) The problem

6) First attempt

7) Second attempt

8) The resolution

9) Looking to the future

10) Moral of the story

Now, create a story in color that your readers can see, hear, feel, touch, smell and taste. 500 WORDS

Note: This exercise does not need to be transcribed later.

DAY 52 EXERCISE STORYspeak-it

Go through your second printed draft from Day 48 and mark any places where you can add STORYspeak (writing in color, anecdotes and stepping stones) to make your manuscript come alive.

Jot down any ideas that pop into your head so you can add them to your next draft.

DAY 53 EXERCISE EXERCISE-it

Go through your second draft again today. This time mark spots where you can add exercises.

There's only so much you can learn about riding a horse by reading a book: Sooner or later you have to climb up into the saddle.

The same goes for whatever expertise you are passing along to your reader. Your reader needs to practice and they rely on you to provide them with exercises that build gently and accompany their daily progress.

You can use this book as an example, it's chock full of exercises, or model your book on the structure of a Self-Help/How-to book you admire.

Chapter 12
Third and Fourth draft

Over the next three days you're going to rewrite your book, simplifying it, STORYspeaking it and exercising it.

Keep it simple

You have done your homework and research. You've written your first draft and improved it.

Assume your reader knows nothing about your subject. Explain every step so that a person who's completely uninformed can follow your directions. After each instruction or exercise in your book, ask yourself, "Could a seven-year-old understand this?"

(Unless, of course, you're writing a book about computers. Then it might be wiser to ask yourself, "Could a sixty-year-old understand this?!")

Approach your subject from many angles. See how other authors have approached the topic, and learn from the winners and losers. Then, make it as simple as you can. Only write as much theory, history and embellishment as the reader needs in order to understand and acquire the skill. You don't need to know the history of the internal combustion engine to drive a car.

One of my editors returns my early drafts with the word "Huh?!" written all over the place. It's actually great. My first job is to "de-huh," or clarify, the manuscript.

STORYspeak-it

Show, don't tell. That's another golden rule of a well-written self-help book. It's especially useful when you need to explain a complicated or abstract concept. That's what I did in the story about my local paper and Francis Xavier Muldoon. I didn't just tell you to go off and write as much and as fast as you could in ten minutes; I showed you what *Writing Madly* looks like in a real situation.

Exercise-it

The same thing applies if you're writing a book on how to decorate cakes. You're not going to merely tell the reader to first "make some icing." You're going to show the reader how to make icing, step by step, possibly with photos or illustrations and then get them to do it themselves. And you'll probably show how to make several kinds of icing, and explain which are best for what applications.

Find your form

Your book structure should be based on your content. Self-help books run the gamut from how to teach your cat tricks, to how to deal with grieving the death of a loved one. Obviously those two books will be very different in form and structure. The first will have lots of step-by-step instructions and photos; the second will not. The grief book, though, may have simple exercises involving guided meditations or emotional checklists.

Other self-help books are based on lists: the seven laws of spiritual success, the ten things you must do to succeed in business. These kinds of books are probably the simplest to assemble from a structural point of view. But whatever your subject matter, make sure your structure and content play nicely together.

Second editions, second chances

Don't worry too much if you don't get everything right the first time. If you're self-publishing, the great thing is you can always make corrections and changes to your book once you've sold your first batch. (Best not to print 5,000 copies for your first run, though, unless you're *very* confident.) With e-books, you can update your book pretty much anytime. Even traditional publishers update newer editions of books to keep them current.

DAYS 54 through 73 EXERCISES Third draft

Take TWENTY DAYS, two days per chapter, to rewrite your book in Color and with Exercises. Incorporate the notes on your manuscript from the STORYspeak-it and Exercise-it exercises.

Write at your own pace. When you have finished, update your Table of Contents, write third draft in the header and print out your manuscript.

Important Tips

1. Getting unstuck

If you're having trouble with a particular sentence or section, mark it and move ahead to another sentence, section or chapter. Come back to the troublesome bit later. If it's still difficult, imagine you've been asked by your local paper to write three hundred words on two aspects of your subject.

If you're still feeling stuck about something, sleep on it or go for a run or do some gardening—just do something completely different for a few hours. Often during that time, your subconscious mind will work on the problem and, next thing you know, the solution presents itself.

2. Simplify your style.

"Keep it simple" applies not only to big concepts and ideas, but also to the small stuff. Short words and short sentences are often better than big words and long phrases or convoluted sentences. Use "start" rather than "commence," "on time" rather than "in a timely manner." Avoid jargon or, if it's essential, explain it or include a glossary. For example, if your book is about marketing but it's aimed at people just getting into the business, you'll need to explain what terms such as "shoptimization," "digi-tail" or "mocial" mean.

3. Chunk it.

Break your material down into easily digestible chunks. Short paragraphs and bulleted and numbered lists help to lead the reader's eye through the book. Sidebars and sections of exercises or tips can help organize your material. Add headings and/or subheadings to sections, which also help with organizing your material into a logical sequence. Create subheadings that tell the reader what's coming up next. If your style is breezy and light, bonus points if you can write snappy or witty headings and subheadings—and chapter titles too, of course.

4. Tell a story.

Remember the story of my encounter with Peter Workman of Workman Publishing? I expect that story engaged you because it was true, it had a mini plot and suspense—will I get the book contract or not?—and it included dialogue. (Dialogue always livens up writing.)

We humans have been addicted to stories ever since we acquired language, and stories are a great way to explain things. Work in short anecdotes or stories that can serve as concrete examples or illustrations of your general concepts or ideas.

If you don't know of any true stories that fit a particular section, and it's been a long while in your book since the last anecdote, make one up. I don't mean lie! But let's say you want to explain how eye contact matters when meeting new people. Invent a brief scenario with an imaginary character ("When Emilio walked into the job interview, he mostly looked at the floor.") You're allowed to do that. And even if readers aren't sure if the anecdote is true, their attention perks up when you begin a story that clearly illustrates your point. It's just human nature.

5. Fill in the blanks.

Sometimes the hardest thing to figure out is not what to include in your book, but what you *forgot* to include. There may be things you know so well about your subject matter that they're second nature to you. Try to figure out what they might be: "Oh, no! I mentioned insulation, but I forgot to explain *how* you insulate a house!" If you're not sure what's missing, ask friends to read your book (after the second draft) and point out anything that's not clear or that they don't understand.

6. Write first, edit later.

Writing comes first, editing comes second. Don't stop the writing flow to analyze the structure of your previous paragraph. Don't engage in a lengthy Google search to find out the exact statistic you're after. Just leave a blank, mark it and fill it in later. Keep the flow going and avoid processes that will interfere with it. The main thing is to get the floor, the walls and the roof up. Painting and cleanup comes later.

7. Invite some guests.

A great way to make your book more exciting is to interview your colleagues and other notables in your field. Quote them accurately and credit by name those who wish to be credited—or you can ask them to write a short section on a particular topic. Most people will do it for free. Even if someone wants to be paid to contribute, it will be worth it to get a fresh take, specialized knowledge or insider tips.

DAYS 74 through 76 EXERCISES - Fourth Draft

> Take THREE DAYS to read through your manuscript one last time making adjustments as you go. When you are satisfied, print out your fourth draft.

Next - Get it read.

Invite two people you trust and respect for their intelligence and their honesty to read your completed fourth draft. DO NOT ask family members and close friends because they know you too well.

Finally

Incorporate only the feedback you strongly agree with and print out your fourth and final draft. Send an electronic copy to your editor, relax and wait for the feedback from your editor. This can take up to 2 months.

If you're planning to send your manuscript off to an agent or publisher, remember to format it correctly (see page 96.)

If you are going to self-publish and you haven't already decided who is going to design, convert, submit and print your self-help book, now is the time to seek out the best professionals you can afford.

Another alternative is to go online to look into organizations like Lulu, CreateSpace and, the one I'm using for this self-help book, Next Century Publishing.

While you are waiting to hear back from your editor, or researching your dream agent or publisher you can put your spare time to good use by making yourself, and your book, more $aleable in preparation for the next part of this book.

Imagine you were thrown into the Publisher's Pit—an imaginary lair where publishers, armed with juicy book deals and six figure advances assemble once every blue moon in search of exciting new authors. Each budding author is given 90 seconds to answer the seven questions that unlock publishers hearts and wallets.

1. What's your killer title?
2. What's it all about?
3. Who's going to read it?
4. What's the unique benefit you offer your reader?
5. What's your fresh approach?
6. Who the heck are you?
7. "When you've finished reading this book you'll be able to…

PART FOUR: PROMOTING AND PUBLISHING

"Without promotion, something terrible happens . . . nothing!"

P. T. Barnum

Chapter 13
Focus and fame

What's this got to do with ... ?

I t's story time again, and this one is about saleability—not your book's saleability, but rather your *personal* saleability.

The New York Times called Peter Workman "the legendary book publisher with an eye for hits." Peter had a profound effect on the lives of everyone who knew him in the publishing business. He was well known for working closely with his authors and editors, and his motto was "no book before its time." His successes included blockbusters like *The Official Preppy Handbook, What to Expect When You're Expecting* and *1,000 Places to See Before You Die.*

I sat in Peter's office for the first time in 1998. On my right, awaiting the verdict, was my new agent, Sheree Bykofsky. On my left was Workman's senior acquisitions editor, "Million-Dollar Sally." (Rumor had it that if Sally edited your book, you'd earn at least a million dollars. But I'm pretty sure no one had the nerve to call her that to her face!)

Peter leafed through my self-published book *How to Make People Like You in 90 Seconds or Less.*

He stopped randomly, pointed to a paragraph and asked, "What's this got to do with making people like you?"

I peered over. "Er. Nothing, really," I said.

Peter leafed through a few more pages and pointed to another paragraph. "And this? What's this got to do with making people like you?"

"Um. Actually, nothing." I was starting to feel incredibly stupid.

On to the next random paragraph.

"Yes. Yes, that does." I tried to regain my confidence.

The process went on pretty much the same way for about five minutes. I knew my book was doomed.

"Right, then," Peter pronounced. "All we have to do is turn three paragraphs into a 180-page book."

I spent the next few weeks doing precisely that—at 1,500 words a day.

Who the heck are you?

But Peter hadn't finished. "I love the title," he said. "I like you, I like your energy, I like the way you come across. But who the heck are you?"

I got his point. Your credibility is as important as your title. People will buy your book if you are a credible, trustworthy expert.

The Daily Gazette will be interested in you because someone saw you on *Breakfast Television*. The TD Bank read about you in the *Gazette* and wants to have you talk to their team from coast to coast and order a book for everyone. And an agent heard about you from his Mobile Mortgage Specialist at the TD Bank and has a client who's a publisher who mentioned they're looking to branch out into the self-help market. That's the way it works. It's just another form of networking.

When you build credibility, you build respect and add value to your words and your brand. So you need to start building your own "creds" today. Figure out a way to get on TV, on the radio, in the press and into other people's blogs. It's called getting publicity. Tie yourself into seasonal events—time to change to winter tires, Valentine's Day, water safety—or anything that people are talking about and that your expertise can address: the perils of too much hot sauce, the skinny on the newest social media platform, the best way to train your gerbil. Invent something relevant to your topic and today's lifestyle, and email, text, fax or phone producers of radio and TV shows, online magazines and blogs, or find a friend of a friend who knows someone who can pitch you.

DAY 77 EXERCISE Staying focused

Ask yourself with each paragraph, "What does this have to do with (insert the title of your book, or the title of each chapter here)?"

Take as much time as you need.

The book stops here

These important yet frequently overlooked connections are the vital signs of an aspiring self-help author. Of the tens of thousands of books published every year, ninety-five percent are by people who have zero credibility outside of their own circle. That's why most self-published authors have basements full of books.

Let's say you're a podiatrist who has produced *Everybody's Guide to Corns and Calluses*. After you've given a copy to all your clients and friends, spoken at your local Podiatry Convention and embarrassed your staff into taking a few copies home, there's nowhere else for them to go. That's because nobody's ever heard of you who's more than 300 miles away, and besides, you're not the first person to write about corns and calluses; Hippocrates beat you to it.

Agents and publishers still put a lot of faith in marketable authors.

Three months before my first book was released, Peter Workman tasked his publicity department to make me into "somebody." The job fell to Stacey, who organized a twenty-city tour with TV, radio and press interviews from coast to coast, which started three weeks after the books rolled off the presses. Stacey made me jump through hoops accepting challenges on national TV and in the press to prove my techniques work, but it was worth it, and I loved almost every moment.

With such a cheeky and provocative title, plenty of people wanted to prove you *can't* make someone like you in ninety seconds or less.

I was fortunate to get amazing quotes from *The New York Times, The Economist* magazine and *The Today Show,* just to name a few. Without these, and without a cheeky title, I would never have built my credibility.

As I described earlier, when the very first self-published version of *How to Make People Like You* was published, I wangled my way onto *Breakfast Television* in Toronto and made an offer to schools. "Put together a class of job-seeking kids, and I'll come tell them how to ace interviews for free."

The word began to spread, and my speaking techniques began to grow. This is just one of an ongoing parade of adventures I've initiated over the years to keep my books fresh and in the public eye. And I'm "old-school." Look up Tim Ferriss on the Internet and you'll see how to use social media and blogs to get you rolling.

With a little creativity, you can figure out opportunities for your own self-help book.

And remember, as an expert, you must be prepared to continually improve and be at the forefront of your specialty. True experts invest lots of time and effort into growing and coming up with new material. This gives you ongoing reasons to keep yourself in the media spotlight, which is always voraciously searching out new content.

Quantum leap your success

You have the resources and the resourcefulness to accomplish ten times more that you ever do, but you are limited. Not by what you can do, but by what you are willing to try.

Your willingness to take risks and step out of your comfort zone gives you access to all kinds of hidden opportunities and lucky breaks.

If you want to quantum leap your writing skills, your understanding of your topic and make your book even more saleable, find a way to give three speeches on your chosen topic over the next six weeks.

You can speak to a group of friends, your local rotary club, your favorite association, a group at work, your kid's school or anyone who will listen—you decide.

Giving a speech will force you to focus, interact, prioritize, learn, build modules and find the hot-buttons of your topic. It will also make you incredibly excited and pave the way to becoming a paid speaker.

Make your speech a fifteen minute Shish-Kebab with a hook, a point, an emotional opening and closing and three chunks of steak and sizzle.

Only a few of my students have plucked up the courage to go off and do this. Each of them went away terrified. They came back radiant.

Feed the media beast

In his excellent book, *Feeding the Media Beast: An Easy Recipe for Great Publicity*, Mark Mathis writes that the media beast likes its food **simple**, **emotional** and **different**. What does he mean by this?

1) **Simple seduces.** Albert Einstein said, "Everything should be made as simple as possible, but not simpler." Offer someone an entire watermelon, ask them to take a bite and watch them turn you down. Offer them a slim, juicy slice and just watch them go for it. Extract all the unnecessary complexity from your book, and your readers will devour it.

2) **Emotion is entertaining.** We are emotional beings. All writing, even the most serious, is a form of entertainment. Every marketing professional will tell you people don't buy the steak—they buy the sizzle. In other words, people enjoy and remember more when their emotions and imagination are involved. It's not enough just to write a good book; your readers want some entertainment to go along with it.

3) **Difference draws people in.** People are drawn to things that are different. Was Mohammed Ali the greatest boxer ever? No. But, he was regarded as the greatest because he made himself different; he set himself apart from the rest with his outrageous behavior, and it drew people to him. He wasn't just another boxer. You're not going to be just another writer with just another book.

So keep the preceding in mind when you approach the media beast, and chances are it will find your offerings lip-smackingly irresistible.

Assemble your sound bites

A sound bite is a precious tool because you can't sell or write a book without one.

A sound bite is a short message, often no longer than ten words, that describes the main idea of your content or sales message. Like your title, it must tell what your book is about, promise a reward, create curiosity, say something provocative, be catchy and easy to remember and roll off your tongue.

You need sound bites to promote yourself and your book, so you may as well start thinking about them now rather than later. Sometimes your title may itself be a great sound bite, as my *How to Make . . .* titles are. Or sometimes you can incorporate part, or all, of the title into a sound bite.

It must be almost like a slogan that your readers can run down the corridor and tell their friends or coworkers about.

"Hey, Donna, I just heard this guy on the radio who wrote a book about making people like you in ninety seconds or less. We should get a copy for the front line teams."

This is called word-of-mouth marketing, and it can help make your book go viral—and viral sells.

To do this, you have to connect with your readers fast, solve their problems fast and entertain them as you go. Then they blog about your book, tell their friends and publish their reviews on Amazon. This can lead to all kinds of further opportunities: public appearances, speaking engagements, foreign rights, opportunities to share your expertise in your community and movie options like *What to Expect When You're Expecting.*

When they've finished reading your book, your reader must be able to say to a friend, "When you've read this book you'll be able to . . . bake cakes like a French pastry chef while bathing your kids," or ". . . play the piano with your eyes closed," or even ". . . shoe a horse in a blizzard."

This review from my book *Convince Them in 90 Seconds or Less* said it for me: *"Nick Boothman's brilliant stroke is to guarantee that within the first 90 seconds of meeting someone, you'll be connecting like old trusted friends."*

Now *you* fill in the blanks for your book, and make sure it sounds unique.

DAY 78 EXERCISE "So, what's it all about?"

Take TEN MINUTES EACH to answer these fundamental questions. **Summarize here, and transfer to your notes folder.**

1. Find a way to describe your book in ten seconds or less, and make sure it offers a unique benefit to the reader.

2. What's my promise to the reader?

3. Finish this sound bite to the reader.

"When you've finished reading this book, you'll be able to . . . "

My actual notes from How to Make People Like You in 90 Seconds or Less

1. **Find a way to describe your book in ten seconds or less, and make sure it offers a unique benefit to the reader.**

How to make people like you in 90 seconds or less.

2. **What's my promise to the reader?**

In the first 90 seconds of meeting someone, you'll be communicating like old, trusted friends.

3. **Finish this sound bite to the reader.**

"When you've finished reading this book, you will be able to connect and find common ground with all types of people—quickly and comfortably."

Actual notes for my next book

(Distilled from my *Writing Madly* sessions)

1. **Find a way to describe your book in ten seconds or less, and make sure it offers a unique benefit to the reader.**

How to survive to 105.

2. **What's my promise to the reader?**

By making small adjustments to your lifestyle and self-talk, anyone can add active, meaningful years to his life.

3. **Finish this sound bite.**

"When you've finished reading this book, you'll be able to break your barriers and make great things happen."

Chapter 14
Call in the pros

What's the biggest change in book publishing over the last five years? Once upon a time, you'd send your manuscript to a publisher or find an agent to do it for you for a commission. Banking on the agent's negotiating skills and expertise, you stood to get a better deal in the long run than you could by negotiating yourself. But that's not the case anymore.

New business models are popping up everywhere offering publishing services on demand. Everything from advice on how to get published or self-published, manuscript coaching, editorial services and marketing support is there for the clicking.

Today, conventional book publishers rely increasingly on a few blockbusters to pay for the flops.

Celebrity authors and established moneymakers line the bookshelves, and the new guys have a hard time getting a foot in the door. Random House, for example, doesn't accept unsolicited submissions, proposals, manuscripts or submission queries via e-mail any more. Harper Collins is only accepting submissions for romance and suspense/thrillers for their new digital imprints.

Another big change is reader reviews. The Internet offers authors and readers real alternatives. Readers rate books and spread the word. This can be a two-edged sword because there are plenty of people who bash books just for the fun of it. You can usually tell who they are—they're often the ones with lots of spelling mistakes!

Agents

The role of agents is changing too. Some literary agents, like mine, still invest their time working with their authors to build long-term careers. But, as more and more aspiring authors find their own way into the market, agents look to find new ways to make their own author relationships pay, such as offering editing and structural advice to writers, for a fee.

Successful literary agents are extremely busy people—with all those books published every single day, this should come as no surprise.

I can tell you from personal experience, the good ones are very hard to crack. If they're too busy to see you, it's because they are good.

Finding an agent

Visit the largest bookstore in your area and take a look at the books they sell in your genre. Look in the "Acknowledgments" section of each book and you are almost certain to find the names of the author's agent and the book's editor. Those are the agents and editors who are most likely to know about your subject and its chance of being published. Be aware that agents' websites have submission guidelines.

The only reason a former fashion photographer from Ontario got a ton of action when he submitted his self-published book to fourteen agents and publishers back in 1997 was because of his title: *How to Make People Like You in 90 Seconds or Less.* It was cheeky, snappy and irresistible. As I mentioned before, even before I submitted it, when I had only an outline, two sample chapters and the title, a well-known publisher offered to buy the world rights from me and have it written for me. I declined.

What does this mean to you and your book? You have to *shine.* Bowker, the company that issues International Standard Book Numbers (ISBN), reported that 3,500 books were published each day in 2012 in the United States alone. This doesn't include e-books, since most are published straight to Amazon without ISBN numbers or other ways of tracking their sales. That's a colossal amount of competition.

When my friend Dorothea Helms, AKA The Writing Fairy, suggested I find an agent, I got hold of a well-known writers' reference guide entitled *Writer's Market* and looked up agents who handle self-help books. I mailed out fourteen copies of my self-published book with a cover letter. I was very lucky a copy landed on the desk of the perfect agent in Manhattan. The title alone sparked faxes, phone calls and two juicy offers within ten days of signing with her—one from Random House and the other from Workman, the dream publisher for any self-help author.

Riding a brand

Publishing has changed a lot since then. Over the next few years, authors will need to be more entrepreneurial when it comes to working with a traditional publisher. Big name publishing houses will use their brand power to attract authors who are willing to pay for that level of exposure. It's called "riding a brand." You want a Random House? If they're happy with what you've written, you'll probably have to pay them to have their imprint on your book. It's just more credentials. If Random House publishes you, the online and brick-and-mortar stores will take you seriously.

Making the choice to go with an agent or to self-publish may not be up to you for a few reasons. First, it gets tougher every year to find an agent or a publisher—unless you come up with something remarkable.

Second, with traditional publishing, it can take two or three years for a finished manuscript to become a published book. Third, you might find, as I did with this book, that your new book conflicts with one already in your publisher's catalogue.

At the beginning of the book, remember that I mentioned I wrote the first version of *How to Write a Saleable Book in 10-Minute Bursts of Madness* as a workbook to accompany a Master Class on writing a self-help book? And for sure you recollect my banging on about the power of a killer title with a benefit. And do you recall the power of word-of-mouth marketing I talked about a few pages back? Well the three things came together and clicked with the book you have in your hands right now.

Someone at the Master Class posted it on Facebook. A follower saw the post and told his doctor, who had been itching to write a book for years. The doctor mentioned it to a friend at dinner, and within three weeks my phone rang.

On the line was the president of the publishing company whose imprint appears at the front of this edition. He not only offered me a publishing contract, but a speaking engagement in Las Vegas, a coaching contract and an order for 10,000 copies of *How to Make People Like You in 90 Seconds or Less* to offer as an example of a self-help book that "has legs"—meaning it's a book that keeps on selling year after year.

Chapter 15
Considering a
proposal?

A sk an agent or a book publisher to read your book today and guess what they'll say?

"Sorry, we don't read manuscripts; we only read book proposals."

Publishers reading every book submitted to them would be like someone expecting you to watch every program on TV to figure out which one you want to see, instead of using the TV guide.

As far as your book is concerned, your proposal is the most important thing you'll ever write. And your overview is the most important part of your proposal.

Its job is to get agents and publishers excited and convince them of your book's potential to make money. Many authors write their overview last—after they've researched and developed their ideas.

A book proposal explains why your book is a saleable, marketable product—no matter what the genre. With self-help books, you don't need to write the whole book; in fact, publishers prefer that you don't. And anyway, as I already mentioned, most big publishers no longer take submissions directly from writers. They rely on agents to wheedle out the winners.

A book proposal typically includes:

- a cover page
- an overview
- the market
- a business case
- the competition
- a table of contents
- a sample chapter or two
- publicity and promotion
- about the author

Your book proposal makes the business case for your book. It explains why it deserves to be published, who the competition is, where it will sell and why it will sell.

If your book proposal is accepted, you'll get a contract to write the book. If not, you have a game plan for your book that will prove invaluable while writing and pitching. A proposal will keep you focused on the message of your book.

Writing your overview

Your overview must get leverage and buy in from whoever's reading it. It should challenge the status quo, shake things up and answer four questions: So what? Who cares? What's in it for me? And, who the heck are you?

The following overview example, taken from my book *How to Make Someone Fall in Love with You in 90 Minutes or Less,* led to a contract and a six-figure advance.

Irresistible Overview Example

How to Make Someone Fall in Love with You in 90 Minutes or Less presents the great news that finding a loving relationship is easier than you ever dreamed possible.

There are hundreds, if not thousands, of books out there on the shelves aimed at showing you how to pick up and play with strangers. Some are good, others even better; but with a divorce rate in the USA surpassing the 58% mark, you have to ask yourself, how much do those guides contribute to a long-term, satisfying and vibrant relationship? And the answer is probably not very much.

Why? Because falling in love and staying in love are two completely different events. But get the conditions right for the second part—the staying in love part—before the falling in love part happens, and your chances of success go through the roof.

In order to write this book, Nicholas Boothman studied men and women all over the world as they connected and made an emotional impact on one another. He analyzed almost 2,000 romantic relationships—from couples who fell in love at first sight, to those who were friends for years before becoming romantically involved. Nicholas spoke to couples who'd been together for fifty years and teenagers who'd been passionately in love for a few months. He interviewed past and present partners of the same men and women to discover what they got wrong the first time, what they learned from their experiences and how they got it right with their new partners.

Nicholas even spoke to gigolos in the sunshine resorts of southern Europe to learn their secret for making instant connections with men and women, anywhere, anytime and without hesitation. He talked with people who had lost partners to illness or accidents and believed they could never love again, until circumstance brought new love into their lives. He gave seminars and workshops to test the ideas in this book, and as a consequence got invited to weddings.

All this research reinforced something Nicholas has always known: that there is someone for everyone and they often find each other when they least expect it.

How to Make Someone Fall in Love with You in 90 Minutes or Less guides readers from attraction to connection to intimacy to commitment, as he shows them how to find the right person for themselves.

Ends.

There are many excellent books and websites specializing in crafting proposals. *The Complete Idiot's Guide to Getting Published,* now in its 5th edition, is one of the best. It's written by Sheree Bykofsky and Jennifer Sander. Sheree is my agent.

You can download templates online too. If you use a template for practice, make sure you eventually customize it to yourself.

You can find a wealth of information at a brand-new site created by my friend Rich Helms. Just Google "booktrailer101."

Besides an overview, a table of contents and a sample chapter, you'll need to include:

Your Cover Page with your name and contact details (or your agent's name and contact details)

The Market (covered in Due Diligence)

The Competition (covered in Due Diligence)

Publicity and Promotion (coming up)

About the Author (covered in Focus and Fame)

DAY 79 EXERCISE Overview

Take SIXTY MINUTES to produce an overview of your book.

You can do it in TEN-MINUTE bursts or, if you find it easier and more relaxing, take SIXTY MINUTES at your own pace.

Put it with your notes at the front of the binder.

Chapter 16
Pitching your book

Once your book is published (or self-published), the real work begins. Your book is finished and waiting to get into the hands of readers.

You can contact radio, TV, magazines, clubs, associations, etc. and pitch them the idea of doing a story on you and your book. You can also write a column or blog, run a website, attend conventions and generally make yourself available. Or, you can hire a publicist to promote your book and find an agent to represent you.

You'll also have plenty of opportunities every day to talk about your book. Before we look at what a publicist can do for you, let's look at what you can do for yourself.

Quick-pitching

What would you say if you found yourself sitting next to the publisher/agent/editor of your dreams on a flight, train journey or in a bar with only a few seconds to sow the seeds of your future best seller?

There you are, chatting away, when the opportunity presents itself. You've enthusiastically let it drop that you're working on a book, or that you've already finished it, and you get the obvious question:

"So, what's it all about?"

There are a couple of ways you can answer this. You could waffle on passionately about all the different topics you've packed into your book and how it's going to change the world and, in so doing, prove that you haven't got a focused grasp on your book. Or you can zap them with a 1, 2, 3 quick-pitch. This is where all the work we did on fine-tuning your point also comes in handy. It goes like this:

1. *"You know how . . . ?"*

2. *"Well, my book . . . "*

3. *"So they . . . "*

For example:

Them: *"So, what's it all about?"*

You: *You know how some* (parents, lawyers, newly-
        weds, barbeque fanatics, bikers, pensioners—
        fill this in with your intended audience) *are al-
        ways looking for ways to . . . ?"*

        (At this point the person is obliged to say yes,
        assuming you've worded the question accu-
        rately.)

Them: *"Yes."*

You: *"Well, my book shows them how to . . .* (insert your
        special, fresh, or new approach here)."

        "So they can/So when . . . (insert the benefit the
        reader gets and how your book will make his
        or her life better)."

If the person you are pitching to has a reason to be
genuinely interested, you'll probably hear, "Oh, really?
Tell me more." Or something to that effect. If you're
writing a book about ballet slippers, anyone interested

in dance will probably respond that way. If your pitching the same book to *Truckers Weekly,* then you probably won't get the response you're hoping for.

Here's my quick-pitch for *How to Make people Like You in 90 Seconds or Less:*

"Hi, Nick, so what's it all about?"

1. *"You know how some people have trouble connecting with others?"*

"Yes."

2. *"Well my book shows them how to do it naturally and easily . . ."*

3. *". . . so they can be confident and get more out of life."*

There you go! Ten seconds on the nose, and I've told them what the book does, who benefits from it and what the benefit is.

DAY 80 EXERCISE Your quick-pitch

Fill in the blanks with your own words.

1. You know how . . .

2. Well, my book . . .

3. So they . . .

You'd be amazed at the number of people who contact me for advice on publishing a book, but haven't yet thought it through.

While I was on a speaking tour a couple of years ago, a friend convinced me to have coffee with a woman in Vancouver who'd published a self-help book about a "terrible problem" she'd overcome in her late teens.

She wanted to help others with her book, so she convinced a couple of downtown stores to carry it. It was a big book—eight by ten inches and spiral bound. She couldn't figure out why it wasn't flying off the shelves. The day before our meeting, I popped into one of the stores to check it out.

The following day, when I gently suggested there wasn't a big market for that particular topic and perhaps she hadn't researched it very well before putting all that time and money into the project, she became incensed. She told me I didn't know what I was talking about, said I was very rude, then stormed out of the café.

She refused to believe a book on overcoming chronic hemorrhoids wasn't going to make it on to *The New York Times* best-seller list!

Working with a publicist

A publicist, whether from a publishing house or freelance, is your connection to broadcast, print and online media, which is essentially how the public will hear about you and your book. Your publicist is familiar with what each reporter, anchor, newspaper/magazine editor, producer and blogger across the country wants to share with their audience. And he or she will help you shape your message and story accordingly.

A publicist is also very persistent. Whether asking you as the author to do something out of your comfort zone (*i.e.,* going around New York City and Dallas to get people to like you, or giving on-air advice to speed daters) or pitching a reporter with a different angle after they rejected the first pitch, a publicist will stop at nothing to get your book to the public.

Let your publicist be the pushy advocate that lands you interviews. That way, when you have your interview, it will be the first time the reporter hears from you about what you have to share with their audience.

Publicists have wonderful ideas, loud voices and the connections you need to get your books into the hands of readers. Trust them and use them; it's well worth it.

Expect to pay a publicist around \$3,000 a month for a national campaign. This should include national and local markets. For this you should get between ten to twelve hours a week, and ideally you'll hire your publicist for three or four months. More time and money is involved if an author goes on the road and is attending events.

If you can't afford this and want to do the work yourself, remember, the media beast is always hungry and the beast needs feeding.

So:

1. Pick your media target.

Don't pitch a ballet book to *Truckers Weekly*.

2. Do your homework.

Make sure you know all about the media target you're pitching to.

3. Develop your pitch.

This is why we spent time on refining your sound bites on page 140. Reporters are busy people, so convince and quick-pitch them in 90 seconds or less.

4. Follow up.

You can send your pitch via email or Twitter or LinkedIn, but *always* follow up by phone.

. . . and pitch, pitch, pitch.

Where do I go from here?

I did my best to walk my talk with this little book. I started writing it in three-hour chunks of ten-minute bursts. It traveled back and forth between Marie Lynn, my coach and editor, and me four times by email.

I printed up twenty spiral-bound copies and used them as a base for a three-hour Master Class I was invited to give for a local writing group. I asked the Master Class participants, to whom I am eternally grateful, to read the whole book in their free time and give me feedback—all of which is included in this version. This gave me a great departure point for getting feedback, then refining and polishing the product.

There are plenty more sales options for me, as there will be for you.

- I can submit it and sell it on Amazon.
- I can submit it to my agent and see if a publisher might be interested.
- I can advertise ongoing Master Classes for aspiring authors.
- I can turn it into an online training program.
- I can modify it for businesses, colleges or schools.

- I can license it to an existing training company.
- I can give away copies at my speaking engagements.
- I can sell copies on my website.
- I can turn it into an e-book.
- I can hire a publicist and get into the media and on TV.
- I can approach bloggers to review it.

The options go on and on . . .

What actually happened is that Next Century Publishing made me an offer I couldn't refuse. They will launch the book in Las Vegas in June 2015 and hold a series of writing workshops from coast to coast based on this book.

Chapter 17
Lucky breaks and chance encounters

Why did I start this book with a story about me, about how I came to write my first book? For three reasons.

First, to show you that you are more talented, more creative, more resourceful and more confident than you ever dared dream possible—*once you make up your mind to do something.*

Second, to tell you that lucky breaks, chance encounters and unpredictable moments are infinite and everywhere; and they can change your life for the better in a flash——*if you're prepared for them.* In other words, never turn down an invitation like the one I received to speak about photography at my local camera club, because opportunities are everywhere—and one thing always leads to another!

And third, to point out that when your imagination is aligned with people, passion, purpose and projects, your potential goes up several notches to where you can make great things happen—*as long as you are dedicated to finishing what you started.*

There's a wonderful line in the movie "Night Train to Lisbon" where the Jeremy Irons character asks, "If it is true that we only live a small part of the life that is within us, what happens to the rest?" That's a great question.

We hold within ourselves the resources and the resourcefulness to accomplish ten times more than we ever do, but we are limited not by what we can do, but by what we are willing to try.

It's your willingness to break barriers, step out of your comfort zone, roll up your sleeves and try new things that gives you access to all kinds of unforeseen opportunities.

Start now. Break a barrier, step out of your comfort zone, make a new routine and invest your time completing these exercises and watch the "lucky breaks" start to appear in your life.

There's not a single best-selling author, Fortune 500 company, billionaire, Nobel-prize-winning scientist or celebrity that will refute this. They know that lucky breaks are real and that they played a vital role in getting them where they are today.

They also know that lucky breaks don't have a lot to do with luck. They have more to do with:

- who you know, where you go, what you do, what you say and how you think
- your willingness to break barriers, step out of your comfort zone and create something new
- a knack for turning bad luck into good luck by understanding that one thing always leads to another

Great authors, icons and artists, from Rowling to Gladwell, Chopra to Oprah and Mick to Madonna, do three things that set them apart from the rest: they challenge the status quo, shake up the industry and make sure people have fun in the process.

More than this, they recognize lucky breaks and chance encounters. These unforeseen opportunities are out there waiting for you. You will be amazed at the world of good fortune that opens up to you once you are committed to your self-help book and can articulate it in a simple and compelling way.

I mentioned upfront that a successful self-help book is like a magic wand and a bunch of ambassadors all rolled into one. I started writing fifteen years ago to promote my speaking career. Today, eighty percent of my new speaking engagements come from someone who has bumped into one of my ambassadors (my books) in Dubai, Los Angeles, Toronto, Switzerland and dozens of other places around the world.

My ambassadors are everywhere. My books sell. The possibilities are endless, and this opportunity is waiting for you too. I wish you the very best.

Now go and write. Good luck!

Appendix

- Three uncorrected, unedited and unprocessed samples of 10-Minute bursts of *Writing Madly*. *The first* from a female student telling women how to recognize and conquer the fears that they'll go broke before they die. The second from a male student who figured our how to make a fortune from your smartphone. The third from a female student who reinvented her life at sixty-three by travelling the globe for three months a year as a professional in-home caregiver.
- Sample overview of *How to Make people Like You in 90 Seconds or Less*
- Sample table of contents from *How to Make people Like You in 90 Seconds or Less*

Example #1

Working Title: The Savvy Bag Lady

Chapter 8 - Finding and being an example role model

Question: Do you feel like you don't have enough education or knowledge to be financially independent?

Hook: You can spend a lifetime reinventing the wheel, or a short time following in the paths of those who have done it

Point: you can't do this yourself. You need an inspiring support group and role models Here's how to do it.

Sub 1) Who do you hang with?

lets do an exercise - look around you - who do you hang with? keep track over the last month the amount of time spent with friends and who are they - then look at what they do and what is their income - then ask are these examples of who you want to be - how you want to live your life and do they have what you want? If the answer is no - then you need to work toward adding some new friends - now a lot of people say they don't want to leave old friends because they are helping them - well folks - I say that this is a detour and an excuse to not be helping yourself - do you realize if you are distracted by helping someone else then you have taken the onus off of yourself to be responsible for your own shit - SO lets say - you spend time helping s friend who is in a much lower income bracket with you. They don't inspire you but you feel bad for them. Right on - that worked well — except are you any further ahead? are you a therapist? do you make money treating others — have you actually helped or have you enabled? - you really don't know what to do because you are not an expert - - but what I will say is this - if you are not spending time on your own shit - then you are loosing ground and at risk for becoming a bag lady - if you spend time helping others or listening to their stories — you will never improve yourself -

also can we take a quick look about how much tv you watch every day? how many new books you read every day? have you taken a course in speed reading?

• you will never learn anything new if you don't make new friends

you must continually be meeting new people in order to learn and in order to stay interesting and relevant and in the know. where do you meet these people - well it used to be difficult — people used to meet in community colleges — now - there is meet up — event bright — facebook events — someone asked me where I network and I said - just look at the event that are posted on fb - you would never have enough time to go to them all - then you go to one and someone will say - I want you to come to my event

- you will never blossom if you keep your secrets to yourself and not share, inspire and teach others

next you must undertake to share your knowledge - what if you are afraid of being on stage and Nick Boothman say - you will not be afraid if you are passionate enough about your topic - so find something that shakes your passion - keeps you up at night and then start to speak about it - see where that leads - there is toastmasters - ad all kinds of opportunities to speak to the public about an topic that you are passionate about and that other people want to learn about - start small in a home or a omwnes club - or start in a a book club

where do you look? Lets do the same thing Tony Robbins does with finding a mate - you need to describe your roles model - a psychographic profile - where do they live? what do they eat? how much money? everything - and then further - in order to attract these new friends into your life you need to ask - what kind of person do I need to be in order to attract these people? in fact it should be the dream of yourself Example,- my daughter gave me this exercise to do one time when we were searching for my perfect date and we called it " you are her" and we actually did it that. instead of defining what I was looking for in a man - we reversed it and said - what is your dream man looking for in a woman - what does he want and here is the list of characteristics we came up with

- gets things done - reliable - dependable

- beautiful, confident, kind
- sense of humour, adventurous, interesting
- playful, fun, easy going
- compassionate, understanding, forgiving
- positive attitude,
- financially independent, good with money

SO make your own list of what you thin your new friend is looking for in you!

Sub 2) finding a role model

Ideas to find public figure role models: top female entrepreneurs - awards - interview them - stalk them - google research them - define the exact characteristics you want in a role model

- who inspires you?

there are a number of typical women who inspire us - arinanna huffington, cheryl sandberg, brenee brown, maybe even hilary clinton for some...

- Who has what you want?

what is it that you aspire to? to lead a big company? to help poor people in third world? the cool thing is that you actually need to state what your life goals are in order to be able to find a role model for you her e is a list of the most influential women on the earth right now at this moment

- [to be added later]

Now you also to make sure that their values coincide with yours - what are your values? go to this website {a special sales landing page to be added] to find a list of values that you can prioritize to see what is important to you - and then you can link up the people that show these value - eg mother teresa, lady diana,

now you have to make that person real and larger than life - imagine how a psychopathic killer does it - hahahaha - become obsessed - as a side note - that another thing that men are cool with and women are not - if someone says you are obsessed - that actually a good thing for a man - if someone says that to you - say thank you - because its an indication that you are doing one thing at well a time and not multi tasking which women tend to do and as we stated earlier - does not serve you well

ok so you need to cut out pictures - watch videos - do up vision boards and write out the characteristics of that person and what they have that you want - it can be fictitious - sure - but it has to be detailed and you need to know basically what time that person gets up in the morning and when they exercise and what they do all day. If they are your role model - you need to know what they do the entire day - hey if you emulate a person who is successful that closely - do you not think that its going to rub off?

Sub 3) board of directors

think and grow rich had masterminds - so for example napoleon hill had a board of directors that was made up of Ford, eisenhower, carnegie and a few other of the most successful people alive or that ever lived and then you ask them for advice. Not in real time but as if they are actually alive and can listen to you questions - ok - its on the borderline of lunacy - but why not give it a go? so find at least 5 examples of people that inspire you and then you must talk about their personality and advice so that you can understand how they would advise you - this will require maybe going into a deep hypnosis - you must try different methods of this for deep accessing - so for example some will talk to people in the shower - I do it on the tread mill or elliptical for some reason - some in their sleep - need a note pad beside you bed and others while during meditation

now you can even have the board of directors debate with each other about what the best advice for you is and how to make a decision

they can help you with how to make decisions - Some members of the BOD will say: with force and no regret - Others: never change you mind - never look back - its the person who puts it off and doesn't make it that loses

sometimes I let something simmer as sometimes it will work itself out - but for the other times - you need to balance the pros and cons - call a friend and then on that advice make the decisions - then if it looks like a bad one - cut your losses

with the board of directors - you need to con-
duct the meeting as you would a business meeting during the day. Buts its all in your head -
go figure :)

you can hold these business meeting at work for
real - but everyone hate meeting but on the
other hand people benefit t them every tonight
like y from synergy of group discussion - as
they say - two minds are greater than one and
then the more the minds the greater the outcome

if you don't have people you can count on you
may - in your board of director have someone
different from you and lie your ideal client -
perfect if you are trying to determine what
they are looking for.

ok this is getting a little far fetched but all
this to say - a bod is required and in real
life an awesome idea - do you know that men
consider a bod an automatic necessity - women?
Ba ha - its a bees nest on such thing - just
start t up and see if it sowkrs -oh its not
making money - boo hoo - I don't know why

Example #2

Working title - SmartPhone Income

KEY CHAPTER 3 part 1 - Why you need to follow
this guide

Question: What are you doing to increase customers?

Hook: Your neighbours kids have more followers than you!

Point: You can now compete in online marketing with and company or individual in just minutes a day

Sub 1 - Traditional advertising

Traditional advertising has gone the way of the dinosaur, as real time news on CNN.com or live Twitter posts have done away with the need to read a newspaper. iTunes and Satellite Radio have been the downfall of am and fm radio use and PVR's as well as Netflix have changed the way we watch TV. We may never again see a commercial as we fast forward through them on a PVR or they're eliminated all together on services like Netflix.

Large portions of Newspaper, Radio and TV advertising budgets have quickly turned to online advertising and more specifically Social Media Marketing. Corporations spend millions each year to get their brands in front of our eyes on social media as most of us are now spending hours each day on these sites through our desktop, tablet or smartphone. Many have had to focus large portions of their advertising budgets on these new platforms just to continue to compete.

Sub 2 - Time vs Money

This age old comparison holds true for this new online marketing. Companies can pay for ads on Google or they can spend the time to write blogs and add new content for their website in hopes it assists in placing them to be found for free at the top of the search engines. The same holds true for Facebook where companies can place ads to show up on news feeds in front of thousands of Facebook users or they can write and share posts as well as spend the time commenting on posts where their brand is mentioned and gain exposure this way in hopes of building a loyal following.

On social media money will buy you the eyeballs to see you products or services once, but it is truly the time you spend communicating and connecting with those on social media that will convert them to followers and ultimately as customers. If your neighbours kid is like most with thousands of friends on Facebook and even more following him or her on Twitter, then you can certainly do the same if you are knowledgeable about what you do for a living!

The great news is that the time you need to invest on social media marketing is only minutes a day. If done correctly, building a following will allow small business owners and even sales representatives to compete with big corporations. These few minutes marketing online can be spent when you have your morning coffee, it can even be spent when you are on the toilet! Find a time when you free from distractions so that you can be most inspired and creative. Use this moment of brilliance to share information with your potential customers. We forget more than we will ever remember, having the convenience of a smartphone will allow you to post your ideas immediately when they come to you!

This change in the way many market their company or the way they tell the world about product or services they sell as employees wont come easy, it not only requires a new thought process but it requires many to create a new habit. Motivation for building this habit is that social media marketing can have unlimited potential, how many times have we seen friends and family share products and services and we have gone out and purchased them. Look at 'Dollar Shave Club', a creative video shot in their warehouse describing their products was posted to YouTube has been since been shared with millions on Facebook and Twitter leading to tens of millions of dollars in revenue in only a few short years. If your content shared on social media is creative and effective, it can lead to incredible exposure that would otherwise cost obscene amounts of money if related to a full page newspaper ad, radio spot or TV commercial.

Not only is social media marketing free, but your followers gained are forever. Whether a 'Like' on your Facebook Fan Page, a 'Follow' on Twitter or Instagram or a 'Connection' on LinkedIn… these followers will always be one post away for you to entertain, educate or excited with your products and services. Respect needs to be given that you never provide them with too much content, or content not specific to why they followed you in the first place, but future your relationship with them and each can be a customer that could be worth revenue for you over years to come.

Sub 3 – Social media structure

The 'social media structure' found in this book not only applies to small and medium sized businesses, but also to the car salesperson, yoga instructor, author, hair dresser and many more that can increase their income by building a following. Just like Coke, Ford and Nike, a following can occur for individuals offering products and services… it fact it can be more effective for those as employees or commissioned sales reps as their posts can create a 'call to action'. Ford may post that a new car model is available, but a car salesperson can post pictures of it on their dealership lot and provide their email address so local residents can book an appointment for a test drive from them specifically.

If you own your own small business then it goes without saying that your business needs to take advantage of every free social media platform, pictures inside your business, testimonials, company history, descriptions and updates of your products or services are all potential ideas for posts by you. If you were creative enough to start a business, then you have the creativity to post and build an online following. This is equally true for employees selling services or products, build your following so that customer wants to purchase from you and not your co worker. Be the car sales rep that car buyers drive to your dealership and ask for you only, be the yoga instructor that gym members only attend your classes, be the hairdresser that is fully booked all week because you post before and after photos each day that men and women in you area want to look like your clients… Build your following so that you increase your customers base, not just for instant financial gain, but such a loyal following that if you were to leave and work elsewhere you following goes with you, providing you with a lifetime of greater income!

Example #3

1. **Working title** - Life begins at 60

KEY CHAPTER 1 part 2 - First things first

Question - Why in the world am I doing this?

Hook - Have I wasted my whole life waiting for my life to begin?

Point - This is not something I want to do, it's something I have to do

Heading - Finding Confidence

Sub 1 - willing to try

I wasted my whole life waiting for it to begin? When you make up your mind theres a whole new life out there. I was scared to try new things. Small steps. I have always been waiting for something or someone but I now I know it's me

I've been waiting for. Now what shall I put.
Can't think what to write o well. I'm brave now
I can see it. I'm willing to try. thats all it
takes. When you decide that you want to do
something different, like being an in home car-
et, you first go for an interview with the
Agency, that's when you have your first interview, they decide then and there if your good
for the job, personality, attitude, personal
life, coping mechanisms , appearance etc. you
either leave with a No this is not for you , or
your handed a pen and a folder full of all
that's needed to start the ball rolling, to
think back to that day is strange, because I
thought wow, I'm going to be good at this, and
I've passed the interview.

Sub 2 - Why am I doing this?

Finally I got done months later, ticket booked,
dreadful thoughts going through my mind, WHY am
I doing this? I kept saying to myself, my
friends we're " oh Becky were so proud of you,"
nice, but , now in retrospect, it really should
have been " Are you bloody mad, why do you to
do this"? So be it, it's done, I leave, you
read the first entry in to the House where we
the new comers were staying, listening to all
those stories about the dreadful clients, etc ,
Well I gotta tell you it's not all the clients,
it's the Carers….. I feel strong. I tell them
good things aren't as good as you think and bad
things aren't as bad as you think.

Sub 3 - Coming alive

I arrived at the incredible 200 year old home
right in the middle of nowhere but beautiful
countryside in Easton, this insane home not
just being 200 years old, it's walls are 3 feet
thick, hence the no signal situation for my
ipad, but thank god the son had sense enough to
get a WYFI wireless network so much better than
trying to sit at the top of the garden in the
rain, or walk up to Picker Field, another fabulous town name, to fine a signal, to make or
get a call one has to drive to the local deli,
sit in the car and catch theirs for a few
minutes, but such is country life, needless to
say there's a huge amount of history behind
this wonderful home, called "Coley Court" I was
met by a lovely lady Janine, who made me feel
so welcome, I got to meet the client, a wonderful 95 year old very much "Lady of the Manor"
the only difference was that his lady was on
"Palliative Care" and that's the reason I'm
here, working with another carer on a 24hr ro-
tation and the change over happened, we talked
as I'd learnt in training, one sits and we talk
about the clients needs etc, and was right into
it, following her with the routine. we had a
really wonderful few days getting to know each
other, and I so liked her, not just as a person,
but her genuine caring nature, and her humor,
I was feeling rather good and confident now, I
learn to cook on the woodstove, so easy and
with such wonderful results, wow

Sample Overview for *How to Make People Like You in 90 Seconds or Less*

by Nicholas Boothman

Whether you like it or not, people decide how they feel about you in the first two seconds of seeing you, or hearing you, if it's on the phone. If they like you, they will unconsciously tend to see the best in you and look for opportunities to say "yes." If they don't like you, the opposite is true.

Harvard School of Health Sciences

In business, as well as life, the failure to build trust and rapport can be insurmountable, while the rewards of a good first impression are almost immeasurable. First impressions set the tone for success more often than class, credentials, education or what you paid for lunch.

Why is it that with some people we make an immediate connection, and yet with others we make no connection at all? Why is it that with some people we feel trust and comfort, and with others, absolutely nothing?

In this step-by-step guide, *How to Make People Like You in 90 Seconds or Less* presents readers with simple skills and drills they can use right away to turn first impressions into lasting relationships.

How to Make People Like You in 90 Seconds or Less is the work of a Master of Neuro-Linguistic Programming whose career is teaching corporations and groups the secrets of successful face-to-face communication.

Aimed at establishing instant rapport—that stage between meeting and communicating—*How to Make People Like You in 90 Seconds or Less* shows readers how to make meaningful connections, whether they are interviewing for a job, selling, managing, pitching an idea, applying to college, or looking for a soul mate.

Sample Table of Contents for
How to Make People Like You in 90 Seconds or Less

True life stories, examples and exercises throughout.

About the author

Nicholas Boothman is an internationally recognized expert in face-to-face communication and is the author of several books including: *How to Make People Like You in 90 Seconds or Less* and *How to Connect in Business in 90 Seconds or Less.*

Nicholas spent more than two decades studying the ways in which human beings connect. He has been called "one of the leading experts in face-to-face communication in the world" by John Tierney at *The New York Times. The Economist's* Matthew Bishop calls him "truly inspirational," and *Good Morning America's* Lara Spencer says, "His book is my bible."

A former international fashion and advertising photographer, Nicholas Boothman's work has appeared in publications ranging from *Vogue* to *National Geographic.* His books have been translated into more than thirty languages around the world.

Today he travels the world over 100 days a year showing businesses how to turn first impressions into profitable relationships. To learn more about Nicholas please visit: www.nicholasboothman.com.

To learn more about *How to Write a Saleable Book in 10-Minute Bursts of Madness,* our seminars and workshops please go to www.WriteaSaleableBook.com.